Tunisia,
History of Governance

Author
Harrison Hughes.

Published
By
SONITTEC PUBLICATION.
2162 Davenport House, 261 Bolton Road. Bury.
Lancashire. BL8 2NZ. United Kingdom

Table of Content

Tunisia

Introducing Tunisia

History

The Barbary coast: 16th - 20th century

With the decline of the local Berber dynasties in the 15th and 16th centuries, the valuable coastal strip of north Africa (known because of the Berbers as the Barbary coast) attracts the attention of the two most powerful Mediterranean states of the time - Spain in the west, Turkey in the east.

The Spanish-Turkish rivalry lasts for much of the 16th century, but it is gradually won - in a somewhat unorthodox manner - by the Turks. Their successful device is to allow Turkish pirates, or corsairs, to establish themselves along the coast. The territories seized by the corsairs are then given a formal status as protectorates of the Ottoman empire.

The first such pirate establishes himself on the coast of Algeria in 1512. Two others are firmly based in Libya by 1551. Tunisia is briefly taken in 1534 by the most famous corsair of them all, Khair ed-Din (known to the Europeans as Barbarossa).

Recovered for Spain in 1535, Tunisia is finally brought under Ottoman control in 1574.

Piracy remains the chief purpose and main source of income of all these Turkish settlements along the Barbary coast. And the depredations of piracy, after three centuries, at last prompt French intervention in Algeria. This, at any rate, is stated by the French at the time to be the cause of their intervention. The reality is somewhat less glorious.

Algiers is occupied by the French in 1830, but it is not until 1847 that the French conquest of Algeria is complete - after prolonged resistance from the Berber hinterland, which has never been effectively controlled by the Turks on the coast.

It is in the European interest to police this entire troublesome Barbary region. Tunisia becomes a French protectorate in 1881, and Morocco (which has maintained a shaky independence, under its own local sultans, since the end of the Marinid dynasty) follows in 1912. Italy takes Libya from the Turks in 1912. The regions of the Barbary coast thus enter their last colonial phase before independence.

Tunisia as a French Protectorate: 1881-1934

French control over Tunisia, achieved in 1881, brings to an end several decades of diplomatic jockeying between three colonials powers, France, Britain and Italy. All three are officially involved in the region from 1869.

The local dynasty of beys (technically subordinate to the Turkish sultan but in practice independent) have in recent decades spent lavishly to modernize their country, using funds borrowed in Europe. The programme, accompanied by necessary attempts to increase taxes, creates profound local resentment. By 1869 it is clear that the province is bankrupt. France, Britain and Italy are placed jointly, by international agreement, in control of Tunisian finances.

This arrangement is inevitably a platform on which three rival colonial powers jockey and trade for position. France and Britain stand together in 1871 when the Italians begin to press vigorous claims (justified in the sense that Italy has more investment and more nationals settled in Tunisia than either other contender).

By 1878 France and Britain come to a quiet agreement that the British will allow Tunisia to be a French sphere of influence in return for French acceptance of the recently established British presence in Cyprus. This still leaves the Italians as the chief claimants for a colonial presence in Tunisia, until the French make a pre-emptive strike in 1881.

Using the pretext that some Tunisian tribesmen have strayed into the neighbouring French colony of Algeria, a French army of some 36,000 men is sent across the border. As they advance upon Tunis, the bey decides it will be prudent to come to terms. The 1881 treaty of Bardo (also known as Al Qasr as Sa'id) guarantees French protection for the bey's territory and dynasty, but it also limits his authority to internal affairs. All other aspects of Tunisian policy are henceforth to be dealt with by the French.

This sudden lapse into colonial status brings many material benefits to Tunisia. But it provokes, through the following decades, a crescendo of resistance.

The Young Tunisian Party is formed in 1907 to agitate for Tunisian autonomy. In 1920 a more aggressive group calling itself Destour ('constitution') puts forward a demand for full independence. From 1922 Destour has the support of the bey. But the French, by a judicious blend of repression and concessions, ensure that there is little progress.

By 1934 the younger nationalists are again impatient. They break away from Destour, calling themselves Neo-Destour. This event brings into prominence a politician destined to play the central role in the future relationship between France and Tunisia and then in the affairs of independent Tunisia. The secretary-general of the new party is Habib Bourguiba.

Habib Bourguiba: 1934-1957

The Neo-Destour party is immediately banned by the French authorities. Its secretary-general, Bourguiba, spends about ten of the next twenty years in French prisons. But thanks to his organizational skills the French never come near to suppressing the movement itself. As members of the party executive are discovered and arrested, others are always trained and ready to take their place.

World War II impinges in an improbable way on the Tunisian struggle for independence. Bourguiba, held in a prison in Vichy France and then moved by the Germans to captivity in Rome, comes under great pressure from both Germany and Italy to align the Tunisian independence movement with the cause of the Axis powers.

He resolutely refuses to do so, but is nevertheless allowed to return in March 1943 to German-occupied Tunisia. Two months later the allies successfully conclude the North Africa campaign, converging on Tunisia from east and west to clear out the Germans. Bourguiba is now able to make direct contact with the Free French, the faction likely to become the colonial power after the war.

He puts to them a plan for Tunisia's gradual progress towards autonomy (gradualism, also known to Tunisians as

'Bourguibism', is a consistent characteristic of his political approach). But his proposals are given scant attention.

The next ten years therefore see an escalation in the campaign for independence. There is another spell in prison for Bourguiba (1952-4), during which his followers increasingly turn to terrorism.

In June 1954 a socialist premier, Pierre Mendès-France, comes to power in Paris and introduces a new policy of partial French withdrawal from two of the nation's most troubled colonies, Tunisia and Indochina. The result, in April 1955, is an agreement for Tunisia's internal autonomy with only foreign affairs and defence remaining in French hands (in effect a return to the situation in 1881). Bourguiba makes a triumphal return to Tunisia and a Neo-Destour government is formed.

Bourguiba refuses to accept his natural place at the head of the new Tunisian government until full independence is achived. But in keeping with his policy of gradualism, he continues to negotiate the next stage with the French government. In this he is greatly helped by the onset of a more serious French crisis in Algeria and by French acceptance, in November 1955, of independence for Morocco. The same is achieved for Tunisia in March 1956.

Bourguiba now becomes prime minister of the new nation, which in spirit is more inclined to republicanism than monarchy. In July 1957 the constitutional role of the bey is abolished. Bourguiba becomes head of state, as president, in addition to his role as premier.

Independence: from 1956

The policies of independent Tunisia are to a large extent the policies of Bourguiba himself. Overall this means a cautious and pragmatic approach which proves very successful.

Relations with France remain on the whole good, in spite of a few periods of intense crisis. These include the bombing of a Tunisian village in 1958 by French planes (the French claiming the right to pursue Algerian rebels across the border); a brief and costly war in 1961, initiated by Bourguiba to end the agreed presence of a French garrison in the port of Bizerte; and the suspension of French aid in 1964-6 in response to Bourguiba's nationalizing of all land held by foreigners.

Bourguiba is also skilful in maintaining good relations with other western powers, and for the most part Tunisia under his rule has a respected role in the Arab world - though his inclination to take a less hard line than others on the issue of Israel creates hostility. At various times Tunis is host to the headquarters of the Arab League (moving from Cairo in 1979) and of the PLO (refugees from Beirut in 1982).

Internally his attitude is equally pragmatic, with a policy of non-doctrinaire socialism. In the 1960s he takes for a while a more rigid line, of state control and agricultural cooperatives, but when these measures fail he rapidly returns to a more moderate approach.

In 1975 the national assembly appoints Bourguiba president for life but by the late 1980s, when he has been head of state and chief executive for thirty years, he is becoming noticeably erratic in his conduct of affairs. In November 1987 his prime minister, Zine el-Abidine Ben Ali, removes him from office and takes his place as president.

Democracy has not been part of Bourguiba's Tunisia. Brought to independence by a single party (Neo-Destour), it has remained a one-party state - though by 1987 the name of the single ruling party is the RCD (Constitutional Democratic Assembly).

Ben Ali holds elections, in 1989, soon after his assumption of power. Six opposition parties participate on this occasion, but they might as well have saved themselves the trouble. Ben Ali is elected president with 99% of the vote. His party, the RCD, wins all 141 seats in the national assembly.

During the 1990s Tunisia makes satisfactory economic progress, but its international image is increasingly tarnished by civil rights abuses. A new electoral law, introduced before the 1994 elections, adds nineteen seats to the assembly - reserving them for candidates of opposition parties. But this token gesture does little to mask the reality of Tunisian politics.

Ben Ali is the only presidential candidate in 1994 (winning this time 99.9% of the votes cast) and the RCD wins all 144 non-reserved seats.

More significant, and the reason for international protests, is the arrest on flimsy charges of leaders of opposition factions, followed by long spells in prison. One of the main targets of government hostility is Nahda, an outlawed Islamic party. Feared by the ruling elite as much as the FIS in Algeria, Nahda is part of the wider emergence of Islam as a renewed political force in the late 20th century.

The Democratic Transition in Tunisia

Introduction: The Tunisian Revolution

The Jasmine Revolution began in late 2010, and resulted in the ouster of the dictator Zine el Abidine Ben Ali on 14 January 2011. Ben Ali ruled Tunisia with an iron fist from November 1987, following his removal of the founder of the Tunisian Republic, Habib Bourguiba, through what was dubbed a 'medical coup'.

Four years after the Jasmine Revolution, Tunisia has made some great strides in its transition towards a democratic political order. The peaceful revolution by civil society and the powerful trade union, the Tunisian General Labour Union (UGTT), had sent shockwaves, causing other uprisings throughout the Middle East and North Africa (MENA) region. Tunisia is the smallest country in the Maghreb, with a population of 11 million people. Unlike what took place in other parts of the world, the revolution did not revert to authoritarianism like Egypt or experience chaos as in Libya, Syria and Yemen. The relatively successful transition is becoming not only a model, but it has debunked the myth of the impossibility of the Arab world building democratic orders. What makes Tunisia's revolution rather unique in the MENA region is that, in spite of the riots that took place in the mining region of Gafsa in 2008, barely any observers thought that three years later, Tunisians would be able to force out the dictator and his administration, or to defeat the powerful, brutal security apparatus that numbered more than 130 000 members. The refusal of the military which had remained a republican institution as intended by Bourguiba, and which was marginalised by the Ben Ali regime to shoot at people partly accounts for the success of the uprising. The will of Tunisians, who no longer feared the tyrannical regime and risked their lives to gain their freedom, was the major factor in bringing down the regime. The determination of Tunisians to achieve their transition without outside interference adds to their credit.

Tunisia Under the Ben Ali Regime

The Ben Ali regime had maintained itself through sheer repression; an impressive security apparatus controlled the population and suppressed any kind of political protest, no matter how benign it was. The regime, however, sought legitimacy through the holding of regular elections which, of course, the president won overwhelmingly, usually with over 90% of the votes, while his party, the Republican Democratic Party (RCD), won all the seats in the legislature. When Ben Ali came to power, he changed the constitution to impose limits on presidential mandates, but then removed those limits so he could stay in office for life. He ran for re-election periodically, basically unopposed, since the other presidential hopefuls were disqualified or harassed. Scholars refer to such elections as 'electoral authoritarianism', or 'new authoritarianism', which MENA regimes resorted to in order to survive the Third Wave of democratisation or to please their benefactors in the United States (US) and Europe. With regard to the economy, the regime was favourably received by international financial institutions, such as the International Monetary Fund (IMF), and by Western powers, which saw Tunisia as a model. The Tunisian government followed the recommendations of the IMF to the letter. However, the economy was not so efficient and corruption perverted its functioning; it could no longer create jobs for graduates in a country where the youth are dominant. Privatisation of the economy mostly benefited the Ben Ali families and their patrons, who controlled most sectors of the economy. Furthermore, the regime opposed genuine democratic reforms under the pretext that there could be no prosperity and economic growth (under a liberal system) without the required political stability. Yet, unemployment increased constantly. There were huge disparities between the northern urban and littoral zones which were dominated by the industrial, tourism and agriculture sectors, and received investments, and benefited to a certain degree from international trade and commerce on the one hand, and the southern and western centres which witnessed far higher unemployment and poverty levels on the other hand. This explains why the riots that followed the immolation of a young graduate on 17 December 2011 took place in the western city of Sidi Bouzid a region that, like many others, was neglected by the government. Thus, the conditions of high unemployment, especially among the youth (estimated at 40%), nepotism, bad governance, corruption, repression, lack of freedom and ageing leaders, which prevailed in other MENA countries too, were among the major factors that led to the uprisings.

The Revolution: The End of the Dictatorship

The spontaneous riots, which were directed by no political party or any ideological movement similar to what occurred in Egypt mobilised large segments of the population. The regime was incapable of reacting to such a wave of protesters, who demanded no less than the end of the regime, thus forcing Ben Ali to escape into exile in Saudi Arabia on 14 January 2011. The military took charge of securing the country, while pledging not to interfere in the political process. Under pressure from a highly mobilised civil society, which rejected the political procrastinations of the interim authorities through incessant protests, the latter succumbed to society's increased pressure to allow for a fully-fledged democratic transition. Ben Ali's party, the RCD, was dissolved and the Political Reform Committee, set up after his departure, was fused into the 155-member Committee to Defend the Revolution, eventually renamed the Higher Commission for the Achievement of the Objective of the Revolution, of Political Reform and the Transition to Democracy. The State Security Division and other offices of the political police were disbanded, jettisoning the last institutional strongholds of the old regime. This process was ensured by the armed forces, who maintained their pledge to not interfere in politics other than protect it from reversal by forces of the old regime.

The members of the Higher Commission decided that the crucial first stage of the transition would be the full revision of the constitution and tackling the inequalities of power, which had so greatly benefited the president over the legislative branch of government, eventually leading to a dictatorship. They also decided on the election of a Constituent Assembly, which came to life in October 2011. A genuine democratic process was thus underway and saw the creation of an independent electoral commission the *instance supérieure independante pour les élections* (ISIE) and a number of laws standardising the funding and electioneering of political parties.

The democratic process also consisted of not only authorising the many newly created political parties, but also legalising the Islamist Ennahda party, which had been banned under the Ben Ali regime and whose leaders had been imprisoned or forced into exile, including its charismatic chief, Rachid Ghannouchi. Ghannouchi, considered a moderate Islamist committed to democratic practices and institutions of government, declared that his party would not seek to amend the progressive Personal Status Code of 1957, which had guaranteed Tunisian women an exceptional (for the Arab region) package of rights, including full equality as citizens and the right to education. He also declared not to impose shari'a law as the foundation of the Constitution. He thus rescinded his initial claim of making Tunisia an Islamic state.

Surprisingly, and to the dismay of secularist forces, Ennahda won the first democratic election of the Constituent Assembly, with over 41% of the popular vote (89 out of 217 seats), although failing to secure an absolute majority. This shortcoming compelled the party to join a coalition with two smaller, more secularist, social democratic parties the *Congrès pour la République* (CPR), headed by long-time regime opponent, Moncef Marzouki, with 29 seats; and the *Forum démocratique pour le travail et les libertés* (FDTL, also known as Ettakatol), with 20 seats to form an interim 'troika' government. The Ennahda's efficient campaigning had paid off. The secularists failed to mobilise voters who still saw Ennahda as the most ardent opponent of the Ben Ali regime, of which it was the biggest victim. Ghannouchi had convinced large segments of society that Islam and democracy were compatible and that pluralism was not antithetical to Islam views that he had expounded well before the revolution.

The 2011 election was generally free, transparent and fair, and stood in contrast to most elections held in the Arab world and Africa. Many factors explain this outcome during the Tunisian transition: a well-educated population, the existence of institutional structures (contrary to Libya, for instance, which practically had none), strong trade unions (mainly the UGTT), professional associations (such as lawyers' associations), and respect for the rule of law.

Another factor is the homogeneity of Tunisian society which, although it has some divisions, does not suffer from fragmentation along religious, political, cultural or ethnic lines, as is the case of Syria or Iraq, for instance. This factor accounts for the promulgation of a national Constitution on 27 January 2014, resulting from a protracted process that met the approval of all political and societal actors. Tunisia's new constitution is the most democratic and liberal in the Muslim world it protects civil liberties; separates legislative, executive and judicial powers; guarantees women parity in political bodies; and declares that Islam is the country's official religion, while protecting religious freedom for all.

The troika government faced many challenges, including a sense of betrayal felt by members of the two smaller parties in the National Constituent Assembly (ANC). They believed that their respective parties made too many concessions to Ennahda, and thus withdrew from the ANC.

During the rule of the troika, a new party made its appearance in July 2012. Led by Béji Caïd Essebsi, minister of the interior under Bourguiba and prime minister in the first provisional government of 2011, Nidaa Tounès proved to be a potent challenger to the troika. The new party, which attracted young people, trade-union activists, anti-Islamists, secularists, former members of the RCD and defectors from the two parties in the coalition with Ennahda, presented itself as a secular, modernist alternative to Ennahda and to those who wished to undo the gains of 'modern Tunisia'.

The Legislative and Presidential Elections of 2014: The Consolidation of the Democratic Transition?

Regardless of the many changes of government and the tensions that prevailed in state and society, Tunisians succeeded in resolving those problems through peaceful means. The assassination of two popular leftist activists, Chokri Belaïd in February 2013 and Mohamed Brahmi in July 2013, almost derailed the transition in Tunisia. But, pressure from civil society, trade unions and new alliances among political parties forced the government to act more decisively to bring about stability and crack down on Islamist extremists. The emergence of Salafist extremists, whom Ennahda failed to confront compellingly although concerned by their rise resulted in accusations that Ennahda was complicit in those assassinations. The assassinations and the catastrophic economic situation, coupled with insecurity at the borders with Libya, tarnished the image of Ennahda and resulted in a sharp drop in its popularity. On 28 September 2013, Ennahda capitulated under heavy protests and demonstrations, and the government agreed to resign in favour of a negotiated technocratic caretaker government that would carry the country through to new elections. Ennahda's decision proved that the party lived up to its promise that it would only come to power via the ballot box, and would leave office through the same process. Whatever suspicions existed about the party since 2011, Ennahda showed respect for the political process in times of triumph and defeat. This also shows that Islamism can operate within a democratic system without necessarily undermining the foundations of democracy.

The legislative election held on 26 October 2014 confirmed that Tunisia's democratic process remained on track. The election took place with no major incidents and saw the surprising defeat of Ennahda and the victory of Nidaa Tounès. Undoubtedly, Ennahda's failure to tackle Tunisia's socio-economic challenges, its neglect of the hinterlands, and the widespread political corruption caused its electoral defeat. On 23 November 2014, Tunisians went to the polls again to elect their new president the first completely democratically elected president since the country's independence in March 1956. The election also ended the presidential system and one-party rule in the country most of the executive power will henceforth be in the hands of the prime minister, who will be responsible before parliament. Out of 22 candidates with different profiles, two candidates made it to the run-off: Marzouki and Essebsi, who garnered 33.43% of the votes and 39.46% of the votes respectively. In the second round, Essebsi defeated Marzouki, who was favoured by the Islamists with whom he had worked in the troika, with a comfortable 56.68% of the votes, Marzouki receiving 44.32%. Given that Nidaa Tounès gained 86 seats in parliament a figure below the 109 required to form a government it was necessary to enter coalitions. Therefore, negotiations for a coalition government were ongoing for 100 days after the legislative election before the head of the executive, Habib Essid, was able to present his government to parliament on 4 February 2015. Ennahda accepted being under-represented in government, with only one ministerial portfolio and three secretaries of state. Undoubtedly, the party accepted this under-representation to avoid the Egyptian scenario whereby the military intervened to suppress the Muslim Brotherhood. Regardless, the coalition that has been entered is composed of technocrats, whose main objectives consist of addressing as a priority Tunisia's dire socio-economic conditions and the insecurity prevailing at its western border with Algeria and eastern border with Libya. While the political transition has been successful overall, the difficult economic situation may pose a threat to its consolidation.

The Economy: The Achilles Heel of Tunisia's Democratic Transition

While Tunisia's economic challenges were apparent prior to the revolution, conditions since then have worsened. Socio-economic conditions, especially in the interior regions, were quite difficult. But the situation deteriorated further with the fallout of the Libyan armed uprising that began in February 2011. Gaddafi's fall has had particularly disastrous repercussions on post-revolutionary Tunisia. Before the war in Libya, Tunisia and Libya had the highest volume of trade between any two North African countries and this grew at an average of 9% every year between 2000 and 2009. For its part, Libya absorbed 6.9% of Tunisia's exports, making it Tunisia's second-largest export market after the European Union. With the uprising in Libya, all this came to an end. In the first quarter of 2011, Tunisia's exports to Libyadropped by 34% and imports fell by an astounding 95%. According to the African Development Bank, these changes were direct consequences of the civil war in Libya. In addition, more than half of the 100 000 Tunisians who had been working in Libya flooded back home. The remittances they sent home an estimated 125 million Tunisian dinars before the war virtually disappeared. Meanwhile, Tunisia's unemployment skyrocketed from 14.2% in 2010 to 18.9% by the end of 2011, undoubtedly due in part to the returning expatriates. Libyans, who had previously visited Tunisia in droves, stayed at home. From 1.5 million tourists each year, the year ending in May 2012 saw only 815 000 Libyan guests all bad news for an economy that depends on visitors tourism makes up 11% of Tunisia's gross domestic product

(GDP) and 14% of employment. The drop in tourism caused the economy to backslide. In summer 2014, the situation was somewhat alleviated because of the many Algerian tourists who visited the country and saved the tourist season. But the security situation discouraged Western tourists and investors to come to Tunisia.

Tunisia's GDP growth has averaged 2.3% annually since the fall of Ben Ali's regime. This can be blamed on the political-economic expediency of the troika, which increased wages overall by 40%, while productivity grew by a mere 0.2%. "The cost of state subsidies to oil-and-gas products and foodstuffs has rocketed by 270% over three years. The budget deficit was 7% in 2013 and is expectedto rise to 9% in 2014. Foreign debt has risen by 38% over three years to over 50% of GDP. Such figures are unsustainable... The explosion of the informal sector, caused by the failure of the formal economy to provide jobs, is now fuelling inflation."

The socio-economic situation has also had some direct repercussions on the security situation prevailing in the country.

Security: The Threat of Salafist Jihadists

Once in power, Ennahda freed thousands of Islamist militants, some of whom were Salafist jihadists, imprisoned by the Ben Ali regime. Ennahda permitted Salafist preachers to exploit mosques across the country as platforms. "By early 2014, 90% of Tunisia's mosques were under the control of Salafists, which facilitated the propagation of jihadist messages. Those messages resonated with some youth, who had been marginalised under Ben Ali and continued to live on the margin following the 2011 revolution as Tunisia's economy struggled to recover." As happened in Algeria in the 1990s, self-proclaimed imams manipulated the marginalised youth who were unable even to read the Quran, and provided them with an extremist interpretation that enticed them to join the jihad against the regimes in various Muslim countries, notably in Iraq and Syria (3 000 Tunisian jihadists are said to have joined the fight there). The desperate socio-economic conditions have favoured the recruitment and co-option of young people by jihadist networks. The youth, who lost confidence in state authorities, have engaged in the informal sector organised crime and (arms) smuggling have thrived as a way of surviving in the destitute areas and/or to pursue jihad. Faced with this dangerous security situation, the authorities have restored the intelligence services, which had been dismantled in the post-revolutionary period, and reformed the police force. The country has also relied on Algeria to assist it in the fight against terrorism. Tunisia's armed forces, however, lack the means to fight the jihadists, who are better armed and are able to escape into safe havens in Libya.

Conclusion

In spite of many remaining challenges and hurdles, Tunisia's transition to democracy is already a success story in the Arab, African and Muslim world. Overall, the transition has been peaceful and the various political parties, civil society, media, trade unions and associations have demonstrated a level of political consciousness and tolerance unrivalled in the MENA region. The main tasks of the new government are now to bring about greater stability, revamp the economy and restore Tunisians' confidence in the state and in the democratisation process. Tunisia today holds the Arab world's expectations and hopes for authentic democratisation. The country has shown the necessary maturity to bring the democratic process and consolidation to completion.

Political Rights and Civil Liberties

Following a year in which the country adopted a historic and progressive constitution and successfully held free and fair elections at the parliamentary and presidential levels, Tunisia experienced a number of challenges in 2015 that threatened to undermine its democratic progress. Three high-profile terrorist attacks in Tunis and Sousse killed dozens of people, leading to the imposition of states of emergency for much of 2015 that included curfews and prohibition on public demonstrations. The attacks also spurred passage of a new antiterrorism law that was criticized by rights advocates for granting broad new powers to the security services.

After winning a significant victory in last year's elections, there were concerns that Nidaa Tounes, the country's main secularist party, would attempt to govern without input from Ennhada, the moderate Islamist party that led the previous government. However, in February parliament approved a coalition government that included Ennahda in some minor capacities. A significant bloc within Nidaa Tounes protested the inclusion of Ennahda in government, touching off a crisis that threatened the former's survival.

Political Rights

Electoral Process

Tunisia's 2014 constitution established a unicameral legislative body, the Assembly of the Representatives of the People (ARP), and a semipresidential system in which the majority party in parliament selects a head of government, while a popularly elected president serves as head of state and exercises restricted powers. The ARP consists of 217 representatives serving five-year terms, with members elected on party lists in 33 multimember constituencies.

Parliamentary elections were held in October 2014 with a high turnout of 67 percent of registered voters. Nidaa Tounes won a plurality of the vote and 86 seats. Ennahda placed second with 69 seats, 20 fewer than in 2011. Three other parties won enough seats to play significant roles in government formation: the populist-centrist Free Patriotic Union won 16 seats, the leftist Popular Front won 15, and the center-right Afek Tounes won 8. Eleven other parties won between one and four seats each, and two seats went to independents.

Presidential elections were held the following month, with about 64 percent of registered voters casting a ballot in the first round. Beji Caid Essebsi of Nidaa Tounes won 40 percent of the vote, followed by Mohamed Moncef Marzouki of Congress for the Republic at 33 percent. Some 20 additional candidates ran; Ennahda did not put forward a candidate. Because no candidate won a majority, a runoff was held in December, in which Essebsi won with 55 percent of the vote against 44 percent for Marzouki. Despite some complaints regarding campaign finance violations and allegations of vote buying, no evidence surfaced to indicate systematic violations or a significant impact on electoral results. International and local observers concluded that the 2014 elections were free and fair.

Following the elections, Nidaa Tounes initially attempted to form a coalition government excluding Ennahda and relying on smaller secularist parties to secure a parliamentary majority. However, following pushback from the ARP, Nidaa Tounes reached an agreement with Ennahda to form a coalition government, which was approved by parliament in February 2015. The decision by the party's leadership to include Ennahda in the coalition sparked a crisis within Nidaa Tounes, which had already been suffering from factional divisions and internal governance problems. In November, 32 Nidaa Tounes ARP members announced their resignation from the party as a result of these issues, though they were persuaded to tentatively suspend that decision days later. In December, another 22 Nidaa Tounes representatives announced their intention to resign from the party.

The Independent High Authority for Elections (ISIE), a neutral nine-member commission, supervises the electoral process. Tunisia's new electoral law, adopted in 2014 in advance of election season, garnered praise from observers as a credible framework for reflecting the will of the voters. However, the law's gender parity provisions—in which males and females alternate within each list, rather than requiring males and females to alternate at the head of lists across regions—attracted criticism.

Political Pluralism and Participation

In the 2014 elections, 70 parties participated. The two dominant parties are Nidaa Tounes, a secular coalition of leftists, trade unionists, businesspeople, and members of the former government of Zine el-Abidine Ben Ali (who was ousted after a popular revolution in 2011), and Ennahda, a moderate Islamist party. Nidaa Tounes experienced a series of crises in 2015 that threatened its survival as a cohesive entity. The party's leftist wing has long been subordinated to more powerful business and elite political interests and is underrepresented at the executive level in the current government. Throughout 2015, a power struggle played out between the leftist faction led by Mohsen Marzouk, elected secretary-general of the party in May, and ancien régime elements led by Hafedh Essebsi, son of President Caid Essebsi. Delays in holding the party's congress to elect a new leadership led to street clashes between the competing groups in November and Marzouk's resignation from his post in December, casting doubt on the party's ability to continue to function in its current form.

The Tunisian military, historically marginalized by the political leadership, remained politically neutral in 2015. However, its budget has significantly expanded in the past several years and it has established its own intelligence and security services. While generally viewed as positive developments correcting longstanding internal dysfunction, these changes have led some experts to caution against an unwarranted increase in the military's powers and its potential politicization.

The government and both domestic and international nongovernmental organizations (NGOs) have worked to increase the political participation of marginalized groups, including disabled Tunisians, and ensure their inclusion in elections. Low youth voter turnout continued to concern nearly all observers in 2014, although tens of thousands of young people made up the majority of election monitors, polling station workers, campaign staff, and election volunteers.

Functioning of Government

In January 2014, Ennahda, then the largest party in the now-defunct interim legislature and leader of a coalition government, handed over power to a caretaker government in advance of elections. Although the move was a positive step in quelling a bitter political dispute with the opposition, it did install an unelected technocratic administration for most of the year. In December 2014, the newly elected ARP was formally seated, and Caid Essebsi was sworn in as the country's president later that month. With the ARP's approval of a cabinet in February 2015, the transition to a fully democratic administration at the both the legislative and executive levels was completed.

The removal of Ben Ali and his close relatives and associates, who had used their positions to create private monopolies in several sectors, represented an important step in combating corruption and eliminating conflicts of interest. A provisional anticorruption authority is to be replaced by a Good Governance and Anti-Corruption Commission, established by the 2014 constitution. However, few prosecutions have occurred to date, with the exception of in absentia trials for members of the Ben Ali and Trabelsi clans—the two former ruling families.

Moreover, petty corruption continues to plague the country, with tax evasion, falsification of documents, and bribery rampant in the civil service. Tunisia was ranked 76 out of 168 countries and territories assessed in Transparency International's 2015 Corruption Perceptions Index.

In July 2015, the cabinet approved a so-called reconciliation law that would suspend all legal proceedings and investigations into public corruption committed under the Ben Ali regime and ease the process for obtaining amnesty for such crimes. The law had not yet been passed by year's end.

Since the revolution, Tunisia has improved its record on government transparency. A 2011 decree requires internal documents of public institutions to be made available to the public. The 2014 constitution enshrined the right of access to information, along with an independent commission to monitor compliance. However, a draft law that would help bring Tunisia up to international standards and improve implementation was unexpectedly withdrawn from consideration in July 2015.

Civil Liberties

Freedom of Expression and Belief

Freedom of expression improved dramatically following the revolution, and the 2014 constitution guarantees freedoms of opinion, thought, expression, information, and publication, subject to some restrictions. However, the media continued to face obstacles in 2015, including prosecutions under Ben Ali–era criminal laws. Blogger Yassine Ayari was sentenced by a military court to a year in prison in January for violating the military code by "defaming the army" on Facebook; Ayari was released from prison in April. Also in March, three journalists were arrested for allegedly defaming the president and other offenses. They were sentenced to six-month suspended prison sentences before being released.

The High Independent Authority of Audiovisual Communication (HAICA) continued to be the subject of debate due to concerns about its politicization and its aggressive policy of fining television and radio stations, especially during the elections. In November, the prime minister dismissed the head of the national public broadcaster and installed an interim chief without consulting HAICA. The body brought a legal challenge against the government's actions in December, but no resolution was achieved by year's end.

The 2014 constitution introduced freedom of religion to an extent largely unprecedented in the Arab world. It guarantees freedom of belief and of conscience for all religions, as well as for the nonreligious, and bans campaigns against apostasy and incitement to hatred and violence on religious grounds. While the constitution identifies Islam as the state religion and requires the president to be a Muslim, no constitutional provision identifies Sharia (Islamic law) as a source of legislation.

Despite these provisions, the state retains significant influence over the internal affairs of religious institutions, particularly mosques. A Ben Ali-era law authorizing the government to appoint local imams and banning any unauthorized activity at mosques remains in place. Following the revolution, a monitoring commission within the religious affairs ministry undertook a campaign to root out allegedly extremist imams from mosques across the country and replace them with state appointees. In 2015, the minister of religious affairs gave the police primary responsibility for the surveillance of mosques. Following the mass shooting in Sousse in June, the state shut down 80 mosques accused of promoting extremist positions.

Article 33 of the 2014 constitution explicitly protects academic freedom, and it continues to improve in practice.

Associational and Organizational Rights

The 2014 constitution guarantees the rights to assembly and peaceful demonstration. Public demonstrations on political, social, and economic issues regularly take place. However, when police responded to a protest against economic conditions in February, they shot and killed a demonstrator. Rights groups have criticized a counterterror law adopted in July for its vague language, creating concern that the law could be used to stifle demonstrations and curtail protest activity. In September, the government began enforcing a ban on all public demonstrations under the state of emergency imposed in response to the shooting in Sousse. On at least three occasions that month, police used excessive force to disperse protests against the proposed reconciliation law.

The constitution guarantees the freedom to establish political parties, unions, and associations. Tens of thousands of new civil society organizations began operating after the revolution, and NGO conferences were held throughout the country during 2015. Antiterrorism and security justifications are sometimes used to circumvent legal procedures for closing civil society organizations.

The constitution guarantees the right to form labor unions and to strike. The Tunisian economy has been rocked by continuous strikes across all sectors since the revolution demanding labor reform, better wages, and improved workplace conditions. Although strikes are almost never suppressed by force, in May 2015 the cabinet announced a decision to not pay public sector employees on days they participated in a strike. However, agreement was reached between labor unions and the government to raise public sector salaries for at least the next three years.

Rule of Law

The constitution guarantees a robust and independent judiciary. However, little reform has taken place since the revolution, numerous Ben Ali–era judges remain on the bench, and successive administrations have regularly attempted to manipulate the judiciary. In May 2015, the ARP passed a law establishing a Supreme Judicial Council (CSM), which will monitor the judicial system. Critics noted a variety of serious deficiencies in the law, including outsize executive influence on the CSM's composition and functions. The Constitutional Council, Tunisia's interim constitutional review body, ruled in June that the new law was unconstitutional on numerous grounds related to its manner of passage and content; no law to replace it was passed by year's end.

In June 2014, Tunisia established a Truth and Dignity Commission (TDC) to examine political, economic, and social crimes committed since 1956. By May 2015, the commission had received nearly 12,000 complaints of rights violations under Ben Ali. However, observers have noted that the selection process for the body's 15 commissioners lacked transparency and engagement with civil society, its organizational structure is suboptimal, and it is plagued by slow decision-making processes. Moreover, specialized courts to adjudicate cases of violations are still nonoperational.

Security issues, particularly threats from radical Salafi Muslim groups, are a major concern for the government. In March, two gunmen attacked the Bardo Museum in Tunis, killing 20 and wounding dozens more. Another mass shooting at a popular tourist resort in Sousse killed 38 people in June. The Islamic State claimed responsibility for both attacks, but the government asserted that local Islamist groups based in Tunisia were behind them. In November, a bomb exploded in Tunis near a bus carrying members of the elite presidential guard, killing 12 people. President Essebsi declared a state of emergency in early July that lapsed in October but was reinstated in late November and was then extended through the end of the year. Continuous terrorist threats also led to near-unanimous passage of a sweeping new antiterrorism bill, signed into law by Essebsi in

August. The bill gives police expanded surveillance and detention powers, allows terror suspects to be tried in closed-door hearings, and permits witnesses in such trials to remain anonymous.

The constitution refers to state protections for persons with special needs, prohibiting all forms of discrimination and providing aid to integrate them into society. It also calls for the state to create a culture of diversity. However, LGBT (lesbian, gay, bisexual, and transgender) people continue to face discrimination in law and society. In September, a man was sentenced to one year in prison for allegedly engaging in same-sex sexual acts, and six other men were sentenced to three years in prison in December. An appeals court reduced the September sentence to two months in December, and the defendant was released with time served.

Tunisia has no asylum law, leaving the United Nations as the sole entity processing asylum claims. Migrants are often housed in informal detention centers, where they suffer from substandard living conditions. Delays in the issuance of residency permits make it impossible for many to work legally, forcing them to take odd jobs with no labor protections. A draft asylum law that would normalize the status of migrants and increase their rights and protections was circulating in parliament in late 2015.

Personal Autonomy and Individual Rights

Freedom of movement has improved substantially since 2011. The 2014 constitution guarantees freedom of movement within the country, as well as freedom to leave. Unlike in some other Arab countries, women do not require the permission of a male relative to travel. The southern border was closed several times in 2015 in response to the various terrorist attacks, and Tunis was placed under curfew following the November bus bombing.

The protection of property rights continued to be an area of concern, closely linked to high levels of corruption as well as a large backlog of property cases. The 2014 constitution introduced new protections for property, including intellectual property, but their implementation has yet to be seen.

Tunisia has long been praised for relatively progressive social policies, especially in the areas of family law and women's rights. The 2014 constitution guarantees equality before the law for men and women, and the 1956 personal status code giving women equality with men has remained in force. The code grants women equal rights in divorce, and children born to Tunisian mothers and foreign fathers are automatically granted citizenship. Medical abortion is legal. Currently, 68 women serve in the parliament. Areas of ongoing concern for women's rights include social discrimination and unequal inheritance laws, as well as domestic abuse.

Tunisian women and children are subject to sex trafficking and forced domestic work in both Tunisia and internationally.

Social, Economic and Political Dynamics in Tunisia

Introduction

Tunisia is the only Arab Spring country which has more or less succeeded in its transition. In fact, according to Alfred Stepan, Tunisia has met all the requirements of democratic transitionthat he and Juan Linz identified in their seminal contribution to the democratisation literature. The first of these requirements is "sufficient agreement" on "procedures to produce an elected government." The second is a government that comes to power as "the direct result of a free and popular vote." The third is this government's de facto possession of "the authority to generate new policies," and the fourth is that "the executive, legislative and judicial power generated by the new democracy does not have to share power with other bodies de jure" (such as military or religious leaders).

Now that all the democratic institutions have been put in place, and that legislative and presidential elections have been held in October and November 2014 respectively, we need to know the chances of democratic consolidation, in other words if the regime seems to be "likely to endure," as underlined by Guillermo O'Donnell.This question is even more crucial as the regime is facing serious crises that cast doubts on its survival capacity. An unfavourable economic outlook and a very unstable security situation have added to highly contested political decisions and economic as well as security guidelines/directions, casting the shadows of a potential deep social crisis.

The political dynamics at play after the legislative and presidential elections of 2014, which allowed Nidaa Tounes to come to power, cannot be understood without taking into account the conditions surrounding the political transition process itself. After the assassination of Deputy Mohamed Brahmi in July 2013, Tunisia went through a political crisis the outlines of which correspond to the characterisation by Michel Dobry: the loss of autonomy of the political sphere, and its permeability to the requests and "moves" from "external" players.The strong contestation of the Troika government, both by the street and by the deputies within the National Constituent Assembly (NCA),was a breaking point in the transition process, signalling loss of electoral legitimacy for the NCA and loss of trust in the political class. This crisis was solved via the National Dialogue (ND), which is hosted by four organisations known as the Quartet the Tunisian General Labour Union (Union générale tunisienne du travail, UGTT), the Tunisian Union of Industry, Trade and Handicrafts (Union tunisienne de l'industrie, du commerce et de l'artisanat, UTICA), the Tunisian Human Rights League (Ligue tunisienne des droits de l'homme, LTDH) and the Tunisian Order of Lawyers (Ordre national des avocats de Tunisie) and has been awarded the Nobel Peace Prize in Autumn 2015 for its efforts.

Through the agreement signed on the organisation of elections, the ND showed the return of the institutional arenaas the focal point of political decision-making, re- sectoralising the political game. But it was primarily an appropriate framework for identifying the key players, the accumulation and the assessment of the political resources and the setting of the rules of the political arena: the emergence of Nidaa Tounes as a political force and a serious alternative to Ennahdha, the restructuring/reshaping of the role of UGTT and UTICA, the exclusion of the Popular Front (Front Populaire)and so on.

Through the transformation of the system of interaction between the players to which it led, the National Dialogue is a very relevant framework of interpretation that helps to understand better the ongoing process of democracy consolidation. What has happened within the ND and the consequences are essential to comprehend what is happening today in terms of alliances among political players, their positioning and their strategic orientations.

Taking into account both the specific cyclical factors of that period (economic crisis, security threats) and the effects of the current context of widened tactical interaction, we analyse how they shape and determine the choices and decisions of the presidency of the Republic and of the Essid government, as well as their implications in terms of legitimacy and the discrediting of power.

We argue that, though many factors pose potential threats to the stability of the government, including the economic crisis, the security crisis and disputed political decisions, stability mainly depends on collusive transactions between Ennahdha, Nidaa Tounes, UTICA and UGTT.

In this paper we will first highlight the political alliances that were formed after the legislativeandpresidentialelectionsof 2014, whichwillallowustoanalysehowthese alliances consolidate political choices and become a supporting force preventing social and political crisis. Next, we will look at the dynamics between UGTT and UTICA, and their impact on the support or the lack thereof of a government that promotes potentially socially infuriating economic choices in a context of severe crisis. Finally, we will examine the security policy of the government with regards to the terrorist threat, which represents its biggest challenge today.

Political dynamics

The game of political alliances

The ND contributed significantly to the current configuration of alliance games within the power circle. It constituted an excellent opportunity for the mobilization of political resources for certain players, which they continue to use, as well as for the legitimization of their roles and crystallization of their specific identities. The national dialogue imposed the employers' organization, the labor union and two political parties Nidaa Tounes and Ennahdha as the most influential and legitimate players.

The Ennahdha party, which was the majority with the NCA and which governed within a coalition called the Troika for three years, saw a reduction of its influence.

Today it holds 69 seats in the parliament compared with 86 for Nidaa Tounes (out of a total of 217 seats).

Without a parliamentary majority, Nidaa Tounes, which had built its electoral campaign on the promise that it would remove Ennahdha from power, today has to live with the Islamists. The composition of the first government proposed by the head of the government, Habib Essid, which did not include any members of Ennahdha or other allied parties (specifically Afek Tounes), was rejected. In the second proposal (the current government), which obtained a majority of 166 votes during a vote of confidence, Ennahdha has one ministerial position (vocational training and employment) and three secretaries of state. This coalition, often referred to as "unnatural," is not that surprising if we take into account the fact that it is consistent with the transaction between the two parties in the framework of the ND.

The coalition is presented as a guarantee of political stability because it forces Ennahdha to support the government in case of difficulties or failure. But one of the most remarkable consequences of the alliance between Nidaa Tounes and Ennahdha is that it has widely contributed to shifting the political polarisation, from that between "antagonising societal projects" which marked the transition period and was one of the main electoral themes during the legislative elections of October 2014, to a polarisation of "liberalism vs socialism" on the one hand and "democrats vs symbols of the old regime" on the other.

The new power balance within the Assembly of the Representatives of the People (ARP), namely the alliance between Ennahdha, Nidaa Tounes and Afek Tounes, marginalised even more the parties who were the losers of the ND, either because they refused to take part in it (e.g., the Congress for the Republic), or because they stood out via intransigent positions regarding the negotiations with Ennahdha (e.g., the Popular Front). They find themselves forced to mobilise the only resource available to them, that around which they created their political identity: the call for collective mobilisation, using in turn two nuances of protest, either that of democracy or the defence of the poorest.

Leaving the political arena to the professionals was one of President Beji Caid Essebsi's showpieces during his electoral campaign, an attempt to exclude outside players and to devalue non-institutional political resources, namely collective action. These had in fact gained legitimacy during the revolutionary moment and during the political crisis of July 2013. The implementation of legitimate institutions should devalue this type of resource in the political arena. As such, the role of UGTT was decisive insofar as the union had often given considerable legitimacy and size to collective mobilisation whenever it was involved (e.g., the uprising of January 2011, the general strike decreed after the assassination of Mohamed Brahmi and the civil society initiative to resolve the political crisis the country was experiencing on 17 September 2013).

UGTT and UTICA, both having gained strength from the negotiations of the ND, kept their positions as influential players in the political arena, positions which have been further reinforced in the context of economic and social crisis. This current delicate situation has created a certain permeability between different arenas. For the main decisions taken by the current government or the presidency of the Republic, the interventions by and reactions of these two institutions are crucial in the game of support of and opposition to government action: UGTT with its potential for mobilisation and negotiation, and UTICA with its lobbying strength. This was the case for example in the movement of governors and the draft law on economic and financial reconciliation, currently a source of disagreement among the political elite.

Start of a de-legitimacy?

Actions by the government and by the presidency of the Republic are assessed and judged by the opposition against the two registers mentioned above: social justice and democracy. Fears of a return to the dictatorship practices of the Ben Ali era are being felt, especially by the political class and civil society. After the promulgation of the anti-terror law and the declaration of the state of emergency which followed the terror attacks in Sousse, these concerns were reinforced by the nomination of a former RCDmember as governor in the latest governors' reshuffle. This choice, as such, does not necessarily reflect a return of the old regime; neither does it constitute the premises of a break from democracy. Guy Hermet has shown, in the cases of Spain and Portugal, how negotiation between figures of the old regime and the new democrats strengthened the consolidation of democracy in what he calls "the impure effects of connivance."On the other hand, a governor from Ennahdha is now included in the list of governors, as is an activist from UGTT. Although the union denies any relationship or that influence was used in this nomination, and Ennahdha criticises the fact that it was not consulted in the reshuffle, it is possible that these two nominations were the result of a collusive transaction, understood here, as specified by Dobry, as a service rendered in expectation of reciprocity which may not be immediate.It is an anticipation of support by UGTT and Ennahdha aimed specifically at reinforcing collusive relationships.

However, such deals damage the democratic credibility and legitimacy of the government. Especially regarding timing, these nominations coincide with the proposed draft law on economic and financial reconciliation,another thorny issue which again exposes the precarious nature of political stability.

From the point of view of the strategic play of the actors, this draft law proposed by President Beji Caid Essebsi aims to ally to his cause the economic elite who were involved in the dealings of the old regime. Article 2 of the draft law states, "to stay all proceedings, judgments and sentences issued on employees of the State for violations related to financial embezzlement and misappropriation of public funds". Article 7 concerns businessmen,who could benefit from the amnesty procedures in front of an ad hoc commission made up of representatives of the ministries and a member of the Truth and Dignity authority. The latter is thus removed from the transitional justice process of which it is in charge in virtue of the constitution. The draft law states in fact the cancellation of the Basic Law No. 53 of 24 December 2013 to establish and organise transitional justice.This collusive transaction, as defined by Dobry, between an economic elite which is trying to reposition itself in the economic and political arena, and the new political elite represented by the nidaists, is meant to give a new push to the Tunisian economy by allowing the restitution of 5 billion dinars (2.6 billion dollars) and favouring domestic investments, but also foreign ones, thanks to the establishment of "an adequate environment encouraging investment and promoting the national economy" (Article 1 of the draft law). That is, at least officially, the justification. This reactivation of the economy should, as a knock-on effect, contribute to the stability of the regime. As such, it should be noted that many economists have expressed serious doubts about the expected effect of the reconciliation on the economy (in the short and medium term). The Tunisian economist Hédi Sraieb, for example, considers that the predictions regarding economic repercussions might be outdated given the risks taken at the political level for such an amnesty.President Beji Caid Essebsi took advantage of the fact that the balance of powers is not yet operational in the absence of a Constitutional Court to rule on the constitutionality of this draft law. A constitutional motion is possible, however, to grant temporary authority for the control of constitutionality of draft lawsto one of the parties qualified to do so, either the president of the Republic, the head of the government or thirty deputies (Organic Law No. 14 of 18 April 2014), who have already expressed their rejection of this draft law.

The presidency of the Republic, through its spokesperson, is refusing to withdraw this draft law despite the tensions it has generated. The draft law has a good chance of being adopted by the ARP, if we include Ennahdha's support, who without rejecting it fully is asking for amendments to be brought to it.The president can also rely on the vote of the Afek Tounes bloc (8 seats), another party that is a member of the government coalition, and of the Free Patriotic Union (Union patriotique libre, UPL) (16 seats).

UTICA in turn supports this draft law, in conjunction with a statement by the representatives of the private sector under the leadership of UTICA, calling for a quick national reconciliation and for a one-year moratorium on strikes.The consequences at the political and social levels indicate the beginning of a de-legitimisation of the current government in the short term, understood here as the withdrawal of wide support which could lead to the erosion of belief in the legitimacy of the political authorities. In fact, the opposition to this draft law from a section of the political elite and civil society is based on a fear of the return of fraudulent practices and corruption. What is worthy of attention here is the resource used by the political parties, namely the Popular Front, to contest this draft law: the street. The Popular Front is using the resources it gathered, especially during the national dialogue, and the identity it built, to call once again on the street, the only resource available to it given the current power balance within the ARP. The deputy of the Popular Front, Mr Mongi Rahoui, said on this matter: "Through this draft, the President is threatening the security of the country as he is pushing people to infringe the state of emergency and to demonstrate in the streets against this law which recycles corruption. It should be pulled out in a pacific manner before the street takes it upon itself to do so."A protest/demonstration against the law on reconciliation, employing the slogan "I will not forgive" took place on 1 September 2015 in Tunis and was confronted by the police, who used tear gas to disperse the crowds. Multiple demonstrations broke out in the regions, under the direction of the Popular Front. On the other hand, five parties

(Jomhouri, Ettakattol, People's Movement, Democratic Current and Democratic Alliance Party) launched a coordination committee which aims to block the adoption of this draft law. The coalition organised a mobilisation on 12 September 2015.

Thus, the coercive management of social movements by the State may inflame tensions even more and thus reinforce the belief that democracy is threatened by a government which tries to muzzle the opposition. The likelihood of the demonstrations against the draft law on reconciliation leading to a social crisis will largely depend on the degree of support it receives from UGTT. It is not a question of whether or not the union will accept the draft law, but a question of finding out if UGTT will refrain from calling for collective mobilisations as a sign of protest. After a consensual position according to which the draft law should only be amended, UGTT ended up rejecting it yet without calling on the street. Its current position regarding this issue is limited to condemning the repression of social movements. Other than sectoral union concerns, such as the elementary school teachers' strike, UGTT has refrained from any frontal positions on the political level, as was the case under the government of the Troika.

Introducing political measures that ignore the process of transitional justice by calling back people politically or economically linked to the previous regime does not in itself constitute a threat to the democratic consolidation process. As we pointed out earlier, the Spanish transition is a good example in the sense that it was led by King Juan Carlos, designated by Franco himself as his successor, and Prime Minister Adolfo Suarez, an ex-minister of the unique ruling party. The Moncloa agreements, signed by all the Spanish political parties on 25 and 26 October 1977, are clear illustrations of the importance of continuity in any process of transition to democracy. The much criticised economic stabilisation plan of the Moncloa agreements was finally accepted because of the willingness of the political class to reach a consensus and thanks to significant popular support.In the Tunisian case, on the contrary, the government must deal with calls for clean cuts with the past as well as political fights. Taking into consideration the Tunisian context, characterised during the transition phase by a systematic rejection of the political players of the old regime, the election of a former RCD member as a governor is a much more clumsy decision than the project of economic and financial reconciliation. Indeed, the economic elite can be seen as having had no choice beyond conformism under an authoritarian regime, but the same can hardly be said for the political class. Strangely enough, this election went unnoticed in comparison to the violent reactions sparked by the economic and financial reconciliation. The transitional justice process in the hands of the Truth and Dignity Commission (Instance Vérité et Dignité, IVD) is an important issue for Tunisian civil society and, ultimately the question becomes: to what extent does a long-drawn-out transitional justice process, and hence the confirmed exclusion of part of the economic elite, constitute a threat to the performance of the state apparatus? It appears to us that, in this specific case, overcoming the economic crisis is an absolute precondition for the legitimacy and authority of the State. For this to happen, the reconciliation must have a decisive economic impact (which is not guaranteed, according to economists) and the government must be convincing about the relevance of this decision. Indeed, Nidaa Tounes MPs have shown themselves divided on the issue and those who are convinced by this option have been unable to defend it, creating the image of a party weakened by its own contradictions.

Recession, economic policy and the threat of social crisis

The economic crisis Tunisia has been undergoing in recent years is one of the main difficulties facing the current government. With an unemployment rate of 15 percent that reaches 30 percent for university graduates (39 percent for women and 20.8 percent for men),a rate of inflation of 5.3 percent,a growth rate revised down for the second time this year (from 1.7 to 0.7 percent vs the 3 percent initially forecast)with negative growth outlook by the end of the year, Tunisia is bound to enter into a period of technical recession. If the economic crisis is a legacy of the Ben Ali regime, it has been deepened by the political instability of the transition phase as well as the existing security threats.

The question now is how the Essid government will manage this situation and to what extent it constitutes a threat to political stability and thus democratic consolidation. This is even more important as most specialists in consolidology state that the chances of survival of a democracy depend on its capacity to create development.For now, in the absence of a five-year development plan for 2016-20, the government is managing the economic crisis on a day-to-day basis. The programme announced by the head of the government, Habib Essid, during his speech at the ARP as well as the complementary finance law tend towards a greater liberalisation of the Tunisian economy as recommended by the World Bank and the International Monetary Fund (IMF). The latter recommends for Tunisia a reduction of public spending, considering that the country must "[a]chieve a better composition of public expenditures by increasing growth-supporting investments and social spending, which includes spending for social safety nets, through controlling the wage bill and reducing ill-targeted subsidies. The recent decline in oil prices provide an opportunity to complete subsidy reforms."Sectoral reforms seem to be hard to control in this exact context, and their implementation will likely be delayed. In any case, they are late in coming and the general orientation seems to suggest more short-term solutions such as the ones specified in the complementary finance law for 2015.

The difficulty lies primarily in striking the balance that must be found between the reforms which must be made, especially at the level of the subsidies fund,on the one hand, and the integration of the social dimension in the economic policies in order not to increase further the public's ire, on the other.

The reduction of the redistribution capacity of the State is a threat to the legitimacy of democracy (as perceived by the citizens). The liberal economic policies adopted by the government and imposed by its debtors would thus be an obstacle in the consolidation process, despite the fact that economic liberalisation preceded democratictransition. Thetheoryof Adam Przeworskiaccordingtowhicheconomic liberalisation does not threaten democratic consolidation when it occurs either before the transition or after the consolidation seems important for the Tunisian case.In the uprisings of December 2010 and January 2011, which led to the fall of the regime, the main demands were for social justice and socio-political rights. The transition period was also accompanied by a noticeable increase in citizens' expectations for social justice, improvement of living conditions, employment and reduction of regional disparities. Liberal policies, without a clear vision for the long term, for now, in an unstable economic environment, represent a strong destabilising factor.

The questioning of the legitimacy of the government is already being felt through the explosion of social movements, especially in the public sector. It would be impossible to list the number of strikes and demonstrations which have taken place in recent months in Tunisia. As an example, the number of social actions taking place in May, June and July 2015 were, respectively, 317, 287 and 272.

For now, these social movements remain sectoral and lack visibility, and the chances of de-sectoralisation are minimal.Such is the case, for example, of the strikes carried out by elementary school teachers requesting pay rises. Despite the battle between the ministry in charge and the teachers' union, they remain blocked. Similarly, the social movement "where's the oil?" saw attempts aiming to transcend the energy problem and its corollary (the redistribution of wealth, raised by the discovery of an oil well in a delegation of the Tunisian south) to raise an issue of democratic governance (transparency). This social movement was in fact recovered by political players from the opposition (Popular Current and the Congress for the Republic) and demonstrations were organised all over Tunisia. But it was unable to come to fruition and quickly lost momentum because of the loss of legitimacy by the partisan organisations in the eyes of public opinion. Besides, the government considers social movements dangerous to economic development. On this basis, the chief of government announced that an agreement will soon be concluded between the government, UGTT and UTICA establishing social peace until 2017.This agreement implies the reduction of social movements in order to encourage foreign and domestic investment.

But this should not distract us from the fact that UTICA and UGTT still have diverging interests, although they were downplayed during the national dialogue in favour of more strategic political issues. Rooted in sectoral topics, UGTT cannot take the chance of appearing to its grassroots constituency as compromised, as elections to renew its bureau are approaching.

After the signature of the public sector agreement with the government on 22 September 2015,UGTT used the threat of a general strike in the private sector if UTICA refused to start negotiations on salaries with the union. The fierce battle between UGTT and UTICA, each one using its political and economic weight for positioning gains, is in itself a sign of erosion of the collusive transaction, which may lead to a deadlock whose consequences for the economy would be egregious.

Terrorism and insecurity: incompetence and authoritarian temptation

Currently one of the main factors for instability is the issue of security. Effectively, 2015 has seen many terrorist attacks claimed by Da'esh: the attack on the Bardo Museum in March 2015, the attack in Sousse in June of the same year, as well as various attacks targeting soldiers and security forces.

The attacks have taken place in an environment marked by the weakness of the security system. It appears that the implementation of reforms in security matters will remain a difficult task as long as the Ministry of Interior is weakened by the different failed reforms due to the polarisation and partisan competition since the revolution.The dismantlement of the "police of the police" (Inspectorate General of the Police) and the forced retirement of high-ranking officials of the Ministry of Interior "led to the freezing of the activities of many departments reporting to the general department of specialized affairs, an important section on the level of intelligence."This situation makes it difficult to control the operations and functioning of the ministry as well as its coordination with the army.

In addition, the absence of a public policy for security may seriously weaken the credibility of the government insofar as the main expectation of those who voted for Nidaa Tounes was the restoration of the prestige of the State and its power.Following the Sousse attack in June 2015, Beji Caid Essebsi declared that he was surprised by this attack and that "the system for protection was supposed to start on 1st July."Paradoxically, in contrast to this admission of weakness, in his speech to explain his reasons for declaring a state of emergency the head of state showed firmness by pointing the finger at the social movements.Social demands are in fact presented as destabilising forces that prevent the security forces from doing their job and weaken the State. The security threat and the management of power over this issue seem to have further intensified the polarisation of "democrats vs caciques of the old regime." As highlighted in a report by the International Crisis Group, the "security necessity" to pause the development of democracy and human rights is supported by the established elites (Tunis and the Sahel), who are opposed to the anti-power and anti-police speech adopted by the impoverished populations and the emerging elites of the south and the interior.The latter is the discourse on which the opposition bases its speech and strategy to delegitimise power.

The repression of social movements can only increase defiance towards the security system and centres of power. The justification of repression via the state of emergency is perceived by the opposition as a way to put pressure on those

who see themselves as the "defenders of democracy" by reducing to a minimum their chances for collective mobilisation and blocking their inclination to occupy the streets to save a democracy threatened by a regime that only wants to revive the old one. The stand-off between the government and the opposition around the banning of organised demonstrations respectively by the Popular Front and the Coordination Committee on 12 September 2015 is a strong illustration of the confrontation between a State which is trying to affirm its authority and an opposition who, via the systematic call on the street, questions, in the name of democracy, the functioning of representative democracy.

When it comes to social policies aiming at reducing the underlying roots of terrorism, the most notable decisions have come from the Ministry of Religious Affairs, which after the Sousse attack dictated the closing of 42 mosques, the removal of radical imams and the prohibition of Eid prayer outside the mosques. However, the minister of Religious Affairs, who revoked many imams, found himself thwarted by his own government in his project to fight radical Islam. The dismissal of the imam of Sfax (Sidi Lakhmi mosque)was rejected by the head of government following protests from Ennahdha. Indeed, Rached Ghannouchi himself denounced the campaign as a "purge" likely to reinforce terrorism. The minister of Religious Affairs found himself thus forced to suspend his decision under pressure from the head of government. Maintaining the collusive relations between Nidaa Tounes and Ennahdha therefore comes at the cost of betrayal of those who voted for this party with the hope to exclude Islamists from power.

Concluding this part

The shadow of an intense social and political crisis on a backdrop of economic recession poses a real threat of destabilisation to the current government. The accumulation of political decisions that are interpreted and perceived as repressive (the anti-terror law, the state of emergency) and as favouring corruption and impunity (the draft law on economic and financial reconciliation) or reproducing dictatorial practices contributes to the strengthening of critical positions towards the regime. Whether it is the economic stimulus or the anti-terror fight, the solutions proposed to public opinion are each time summed up in a condemnation of collective action.

What is at play today is the confrontation between two types of resources: institutional resources versus collective action. At the moment, the second is devalued and the State is managing social movements in a coercive manner, but this power balance is dependent on the stability of the collusive relationship between the State and UGTT (thus maintaining the differentiation between the political arena and the union arena).

Although the government is highly contested, it is only in case of loss of support by both key players, Ennahdha and UGTT one at the political level (vote on laws within the ARP) and the other through its ability to contain social contestation that we might find ourselves in a situation where we risk a loss of legitimacy of the government.

In short, the president of the Republic and the government are on the back foot. They must undertake major reforms and make difficult decisions in the political, economic and security sectors while avoiding the effects of an already maximal risk of social subversion. Moreover, maintaining collusive relations that provide important political support is often done at the expense of compromise (as shown by the case of the dismissal of imams) or is seen as an admission of weakness (as is the case in the face of UGTT), which might increase popular ire and discredit the regime. The stability of these relations is still the safest way to secure a stable government, but this should go hand in hand with a rapid implementation of economic and security reforms and a consolidation of the party ranks of Nidaa Tounes, which too closely resembles a catch-all party struggling with internal conflicts.

Youth Empowerment Can Sustain Tunisia's Democratic Consolidation

This paper focuses on youth contribution within the process of the transition to democracy in Tunisia, with the aim of describing how youth empowerment is the key to sustaining the consolidation of democracy and avoiding the risk of regression.

Recently many analysts and experts have focused their attention on the connection between the worsening of the situation of Arab youths and the rise of Islamic radicalisation among them. The issue of foreign fighters joining the Islamic State or other terrorist groups represents only the tip of the iceberg, since a growing number of young Arabs are increasingly involved in illegal activities.

Youth empowerment is the main way to deter this emerging trouble, which poses a serious threat to the stability of many countries, primarily those that have successfully deployed a democratic system. Against this backdrop, Tunisia is rightly considered to be the Arab country that has achieved the greatest results on the path towards democracy among those countries who experienced the so- called Arab Spring.At the same time, it is the country that presents the greatest contrast between active youth engagement in the revolution and improvement of their situation.

The national government, as well as a large part of civil society, is aware that youth empowerment represents a critical challenge upon which the resilience of the democratic achievements may depend. Almost all stakeholders agree on the fact that building a more inclusive new generation, and providing them with opportunities and education, will create a bulwark against the pressure of internal and external potentially subversive groups whose aims are to divert Tunisia from its path towards modernity. But the struggle is still not being tackled with the tailored approach it needs and politicians are striving to find an adequate solution. Many policies and initiatives have been launched recently with the objective of dealing with youth-related issues such as unemployment, marginalisation and social exclusion. But the effectiveness of such policies is extremely weak, as shown by the worsening data from many indicators. Tangible and effective policies are lacking and a sense of detachment is rising, which could pave the way for unpredictable and dangerous perspectives. Some clues of a regression scenario are already showing themselves on the ground. For instance, in January violent riots occurred with groups of young Tunisians demanding more opportunities and job policies. This has created a negative backlash for the domestic political equilibrium of the country and fuelled attempts by some discontented political members to slowly delegitimise the current government. In response, the ruling party is accused of silencing social movements and opposition manifestations by resorting to the justification of national security concerns.

Externally the country is also on the verge of collapse and, given the already mentioned rise in the problem of young foreign fighters, the fear of terrorist attack is high. The three big terrorist attacks within the country have highlighted the oppositionof   ISandthe

Salafistgrouptowardsanypoliticalandsocialbreakthroughs   and hopes of modernity. Although Tunisia demonstrated to the world that it is a resilient society during the revolution, its success will be determined on its capacity to face the scale of pressure it may have to deal with.

In this vein, this paper argues that in Tunisia the best strategy to improve the resilience of democratic achievements is to invest in youth empowerment.It urges the national government as well as the international community to strengthen their commitment through a more structured and tailored approach to deal with the issue, on whose outcome the stability of Tunisia, and even of the region as a whole, might ultimately depend.

The first section briefly depicts the democratic improvement achieved by Tunisia and highlights elements of strength and weakness that have emerged in the past five years. The second part lays out the events since the beginning of the revolution, focusing especially on the youth commitment in making the revolution goals effective and the tools they used in accelerating it. Also presented in this section is the transition process prior to the 2014 Tunisian Constitution. It also addresses

the ongoing deterioration of the socioeconomic situation of the Tunisian youth. The third part introduces the European Union action in Tunisia, assessing what may be needed to facilitate the consolidation of democracy in the North African country. In the last section the paper offers some recommendations to the national government.

Between consolidation and crisis, the Tunisian democracy

Following the launch of the Tunisian Constitution in January 2014, along with the presidential and national elections, Tunisia has met all the requirements to accomplish its democratic transition. The endeavours of the two major parties to form a National unity government have demonstrated an awareness of political cooperation as the key pillar to bestowing Tunisia with stability. Furthermore the emergence of a more active and engaged civil society, which has assumed the role of guardian within the electoral rounds has guaranteed transparency and, in turn, has attracted the attention of the international community.The country has thus begun its democratic consolidation process.

Among the most prominent scholars of democracy and democratic transition processes, there is debate over the components necessary for defining consolidation progress. According to Morlino, a new Constitution, shared among parties and organisations, may be the sign of the beginning of the consolidation process.If we apply Gunther's theory, according to whom in a democracy the higher the awareness among a significant political group that the institutions are the only arena for political debate, the higher the level of democratic consolidation,Tunisia shows indicators of being a young and unstable democracy. Tunisia is at the initial stage of consolidating its democracy but it is far from having achieved what has been stated by Linz as a consolidated democracy, "in which none of the major political actors, parties, or organized interests, forces, or institutions consider that there is any alternative to democratic processes to gain power, and [...] no political institution or group has a claim to veto the action of democratically elected decision makers."

The risk of regression to a crisis situation could be around the corner. Indeed, the political internal balance has been challenged by skirmishes which have often taken over the role of institutions and the political sphere, even escalating into criminal actions such as the political assassination of prominent secular leader Chokri Belaid on 6 February 2013 and the murder of leftist leader Mohamed Brahmi in late July 2013.Furthermore, between 2012 and 2015, the country has lived through escalations in tension among the political parties, very often reaching breaking points which has raised concerns about the sustainability of the system. Particularly in late 2014 when the national elections were held, analysts claimed it to be a period of "national cold war".The most recent outbreak of unrest happened in mid-January 2016, when social protests were sparked off across the country, by rising numbers of complaints against the high level of unemployment in Tunisia and the lack of response from the government.

Despite rising tensions, Tunisians are highly aware of the risks association with such escalation and, until now, the existence of a broad political coalition has been a bulwark against regression to conflict. The country's Constituent National Assembly is led by a coalition of parties, with Islamist party Ennahda and secular party Nidaa Tounes at the helm, which have overcome their historical contrast. The Free Patriotic Union party, headed by football club magnate and former presidential hopeful Slim Riahi, and the liberal party Afek Tounes are also represented.

In an interview released in September 2015, Prime Minister Essid reinforced his hope that 2016 will be the year in which the government will at last succeed in deploying the policy package that Tunisia is in need of, and in consolidating its democracy as much as possible. Essid has set down the Tunisian government's challenges for a five-year term from 2016 to 2020. The head of government touched on issues concerning the administration, the fiscal sector, justice and economy, foreign investments and security.

However he did not directly address the main issue which plagues the country: the situation of young Tunisians and the high level of youth unemployment. Perhaps it was deliberately not mentioned by the government because it is considered the most problematic issue. This approach has long been used by the Tunisian authorities. As shown by Paciello and Pioppi public authorities very seldom refer to the unemployment of graduates as a problem, preferring more neutral expressions such as "the question of the employment of graduates."Alongside enthusiastic claims, public authorities have either avoided mentioning alarming data on youth unemployment or publicised lower figures.

Nevertheless, following the social unrest that occurred in January, the core of which was the discontent of the young unemployed Tunisian, Essid made an official declaration to deter the escalation of the protests. He warned of the risks of regression and the breakdown of democracy, raising concerns about the infiltration of people seeking to destroy the democratic transition. He concluded saying that "there has been huge political progress but we acknowledge that there are lots of economic difficulties. We will respond to young people's economic demands but we need a bit of time for that."

The plight of the country and the difficulty of finding a solution for it creates a national paradox. If the government aims at consolidating the country's democracy in the coming years by proposing an innovative series of reforms without prioritising the empowerment of youth, it will inexorably fail by being hampered by young Tunisians' discontent.

The contribution of young Tunisians to the Jasmine Revolution and the transition process

Tunisian youth was at the forefront of the revolution from the beginning. The event which led to it was triggered by a young man. Youths crowded onto the streets and protested against the regime. They shared information and videos on social networking sites, which woke up a sleeping country. The youth were active in the process of transition and their engagement is still crucial, as without it the country will be unable to accomplish its democratic consolidation.

From the streets to the Constitution: transition to democracy

During the Ben Ali regime, between 1987 and 2011, any form of dissent was silenced and rigid control was exercised over the media. Gradually Ben Ali and his establishment took control of all aspects of ordinary life, leaving the appearance of a pluralistic system, the effectiveness of which was tarnished by the lack of true democracy. Beatrice Hibou has compared the regime to a Police state to the extent that it seemed "un système et des modes de régulation qui permettent le contrôle de la conduite des gens."

When the global economy worsened in 2008, the backlash of the international crisis impacted negatively on the Tunisian domestic economy, revealing a country unprepared to deal with an economic downturn and too dependent on direct

foreign investments.The country was facing a national emergency, but the disengagement of the people in social and political affairs and the lack of freedom and information were obstacles that created a stalemate. Tunisia was like a large car stalled in the mud. Suddenly the engine was restarted by the youth, whose mobilisation ultimately contributed to launching region-wide protests. When a 26 year old vendor from the Kasserine region set himself on fire, many young Tunisians crowded onto the streets all over the country. Ben Ali's reaction was extreme. He placed snipers on roofs with the purpose of deterring the demonstrations. This action was aimed at discouraging the escalation of the protest, but it turned out to be a fundamental mistake.

Indeed the courage of Tunisia's younger generation, who challenged the ruthlessness of the regime, overcame the fear felt by other groups of being hurt or killed in demonstrations. Moreover young commitment in the revolution caused the bulk of the military forces to give up their role as guardians of a dying regime and to protect the demonstrators instead. The broad engagement of youth in the demonstrations was a turning point which encouraged many groups to enter the fight. As noted by Honwana "The key actors in this revolution were Mohamed Bouazizi, young cyber activists, young unemployed graduates, and civil society groups, including the trade union movement, lawyers, and opposition parties that joined as the conflict escalated."In the polls that followed in the immediate aftermath of revolution, a large number of respondents affirmed that the revolution had been brought about by young people.

The second important mainstay which highlights how young Tunisians were the wind of the revolution was their role in the diffusion of information throughout a geographically disaggregated country. As mentioned above, Tunisia in late 2010 was among the worst countries in the world in terms of freedom of the press.All the mass media was under the strict control of Ben Ali's cohorts, but one: the youngest social network, Facebook. At that time, the largest group of Facebook users in

Tunisia consisted of those between 18 and 24 years of age (39 percent).In response Ben Ali tried to increase the regime's control over every social network, but he failed to see the potential of Facebook and its threefold capacity of

communication (one to one; one to many; many to one)which played a relevant role in accelerating the diffusion of news and images throughout the country. The advantage of remaining anonymous meant users overcame their fear of punishment by the regime. Moreover, as social unrest escalated, Ben Ali ordered a curfew and Facebook became the only tool to share real time events and to organise demonstrations. Indeed Facebook not only played a crucial role in connecting even the most marginalised regions of the country, helping them to be informed in real-time about events, but it also spread the bond of "collective identity based on empathy."In this regard, one of the milestones on Facebook was the sharing of videos of the military refusing to shoot upon the demonstrators.

The last attempts to save the regime highlighted how Ben Ali was aware of the centrality of the youth within the revolution, who were expressing grievances towards the regime that went far beyond the concerns of their age group only. Indeed, when the government understood that the situation was no longer under control and the only solution open to them was to calm the anger of the youth, the development minister was ordered to meet their claims by announcing a package of urgent measures aimed at appeasing youth discontent. But the protest, which had escalated into riots, continued and Ben Ali began to feel under real pressure. Forced into a corner, his regime promised the creation of 300,000 jobs in two years, but the distrust of the regime had reached breaking point.

Ben Ali fled the country on 14 January 2011 and young Tunisians were at the forefront of the transition in the immediate aftermath of the revolution. Many youth associations flourished and it was clear that following the inception of the first interim government the biggest challenge was to satisfy young Tunisians' demand for more opportunities. But even those coalitions who tried to address their needs were at best only able to set-up palliative measures or temporary concessions, which were seen as unstructured and without any long term strategy. For instance, the first interim government, formed in the immediate aftermath of Ben Ali's ousting, was accused of being a fully-fledged revival of Ben Ali's former regime. The unity government that was announced on 17 January included twelve members of the ruling RCD, the leaders of three opposition parties, three representatives from the Tunisian General Labour Union and other representatives of civil society, including the blogger Slim Amamou. The coalition had problems since its inception. Just one day after its formation, the three members of the UGTT and Ben Jafaar resigned, claiming that they had "no confidence" in a government that still featured members of the RCD party that ruled under Ben Ali.

Young Tunisians harshly opposed the first interim government and the following reshuffles were often accused of being connected to Ben Ali's former regime. A proverb started to circulate and became the cornerstone of Tunisians' discontent: "we cut off the head of the beast, but the beast is still very much alive."

The Constitution. Start of consolidation or youth betrayal?

In January 2014, after two years of intense bargaining, Tunisia was presented with a new Constitution.The role of young Tunisians in fostering its birth is enshrined in article 8: "Youth are an active force in building the nation. The state seeks to provide the necessary conditions for developing the capacities of youth and realizing their potential, supports them to assume responsibility, and strives to extend and generalize their participation in social, economic, cultural and political development."Officially young Tunisians were considered not only as a group to cherish, but a national asset in building the nation. Other constitutions of the region do not explicitly mention young generations in these terms. For instance, the Constitution of the Arab Republic of Egypt, adopted in 2014 under Al Sisi, did not pay particular attention to the youth. However, if we look at Tunisia from 2014 to the present, article 8 has not been honoured. The young generation is neither a relevant force in the political system nor a group to which policies are addressed.

Official data on the situation of youth is extremely negative. According to the 2015 African Economic Outlook for Tunisia, the youth unemployment rate is 33.2 percent for 15-25 year olds. If we consider the category of 15-29 year olds the rate increases, reaching peaks of 50 percent, depending on the region.The bulk of them are skilled or graduates, who cannot gain access to the job market. Many unemployed young graduates feel themselves forced to find work in the illegal sector. Some of them also become involved in the cross-border smuggling trade with nearby countries such as Libya and Algeria, while others decide to migrate to Europe. Among the youth there is widespread complaint about the absence of clear strategies to guarantee any long-term job security, and this causes disillusion

concerning the government's ability to address their problems. Furthermore with no stake in society they are prepared to engage in violence out of sheer desperation.

Disengagement and detachment from political and social affairs is high. A small number of young Tunisians are active members of civil society organisations. Except for mobilising demonstrations young Tunisians are not involved in political participation, especially in rural areas. This astonishing level of disaffection towards institutions is very difficult to manage. They have also been increasingly detached by unfair treatment and police violence which has fueled their distrust, leading to an increase in their loyalty to institutions such as family and local religions. The local Imam is often seen as more reliable than the military.

The press is still manipulated and the Internet is one of the most trusted means both to get independent information and to look for a job, especially in rural areas where 45.9 percent of internet use is for job purposes. This has created a virtual citizenship who has lost contact with the country and its institutions.

The education system is also affected by flaws. Young Tunisians are the most educated within the region, but there is a growing rate of school dropouts, the rise of which may be rooted in the lack of employment and the perception of schools as a waste of time. Concerns raised by experts refer to the absence of students' voices in defining solutions for themselves.

Many young people complain about the limited number of jobs in the public sector in Tunisia as well as the lack of entrepreneurial policies. Given the limited access to credit and widespread corruption, private businesses are discouraged. In a recent survey the most evident barriers to growth complained of by Tunisians were political instability, administrative inefficiency, restricted access to finance, corruption and extortion, difficulty in obtaining electricity, weak contract enforcement and weak networking.Young women particularly are a group who have been held back by unemployment and the ongoing difficulties. In many internal areas of the country more than 80 percent of them are not working or studying.

This is the situation faced by Tunisian youth today. An immense sense of frustration merged with disaffection and detachment are feelings which are shared more and

more among the young. Monica Marks has recently said "Many Tunisian young people describe this desperate feeling of suffocation and social exclusion with one word, hugra. This word, loosely translating to spurning or exclusion, conveys a deep sense of humiliation."Their contribution in the transition to democracy has been forgotten and their potential of being relevant actors in democratic consolidation has been neglected.

If the situation worsened or a breaking point such as the Bouazizi event occurred again, Tunisia could fall into a regression phase. But this time any clashes could become unpredictable, possibly escalating into a battle of all against all, as quoted by a political commander who warned that a new revolution in Tunisia will not be between people and government but between people and people.Such a worrying and unwelcomed perspective actually presents some clues, which once again put the young at the forefront of a situation on which the future of Tunisia highly depends. Indeed young Tunisians represent the largest group of foreign fighters who have joined IS to be trained and then return to their country.The International Center for the Study of Radicalization and Political Violence has estimated that Tunisia has fueled IS with young at a constant pace, reaching a total of three thousand.Despite representing a tiny part of the majority of young Tunisians, the phenomenon is a direct outcome of social exclusion and youth disillusionment. For example, if we look into the mind of a young Tunisian, most likely a graduate, who does not see any future prospects and lives in a backward interior region, whose empowerment is evidently not on the political agenda, it is normal that he or she will begin to distrust the government and to rely more upon his local community. He can then fall into the hands of radical Imams who will fuel his mind with misleading religious ideas, giving him an alternative path to follow, to feel of use.

Looking at the past, we have a clear example in Algeria when the economic difficulties of the mid to late 1980s coincided with the large scale rise of radical Islamism, as many middle-class educated young people found themselves jobless and without prospects. Radical Islam offered an alternative that was more culturally authentic than imported Western ideologies such as socialism.

European Union action in Tunisia

The European Union has welcomed the democratic improvements led by Tunisia since the Jasmine Revolution. The country has revealed its uniqueness within an unstable region and for this reason has been the favoured partner to deploy a new neighbourhood policy.

It is difficult today to defend the old idea of an undifferentiated European Neighbourhood Policy (ENP) and, accordingly, Europe needs to be more strategic and pragmatic in addressing the new realities of its neighbours. For instance, Europe should contribute to a more stable MENA neighbour by supporting those countries that demonstrate willingness and collaboration and, in turn, where its actions have a real chance of success.Tunisia is best-suited Mediterranean country for successful external action by the European Union, being at the forefront of democratic transition and consolidation in the Arab World, and it could play a strategic role within the EU neighbourhood.

But time is passing and the situation is worsening, especially considering the new threats which are emerging in the Middle East and North Africa. As mentioned above, the risk of a collapse in Tunisia remains high due to internal political tensions, socioeconomic pressure, terrorist threats and regional dynamics – first and foremost instability in neighboring Libya – that together pose new challenges and call for a carefully considered European involvement on the ground. In this regard, in late 2013 relations between the European Union and Tunisia were strengthened with the launch of the Action plan 2013-2017, whose purpose is "to strengthen the ties between them and promote stability, security and prosperity on the basis of a partnership based on solidarity and common interests."It promotes a set of priorities which should be addressed by Europe such as administration, justice, human rights, economy, infrastructure, competitiveness and security. Furthermore, the EU and Tunisia have created a "partenariat privilégié"which aims at sustaining Tunisia's consolidation of democracy. Youth-related problems barely receiving a mention, policies are affected by rhetorical narrative and solutions are proposed in general terms and do not consider the worsening of conditions since 2013.

Europe still lacks a sound strategy addressed to youth empowerment in Tunisia. Therefore, it should strengthen its support strategy to the national government as much as possible in the deployment of a reform process, by cooperating closely over the most relevant issues. A more youth-sensitive approach should be used, as noted recently by Isabel Schäfer, who said that "the role of the EU is not to tell the youth how to proceed, but merely to offer tools that allow young people to deal with their specific situation."

There are two alternatives by which the European Union can intervene to improve the situation of the youth. The first is to increase the Tunisian government's effectiveness in leading its program of youth empowerment, by providing resources, assistance and highly qualified personnel where needed. In this regard the following actions should be taken:

Create a permanent bilateral conversation at the institutional level, aimed at assessing the condition of young Tunisians year-on-year as a crucial means to monitor tailored policies and their outcome.

Strengthen the cooperation within the educational sector by further encouraging cultural exchange even at secondary school level. The possibility to be more integrated in the European context would broaden chances to find work both in Europe or elsewhere. Moreover it would allow Tunisians to consider Europe as an opportunity and not as a constraint, replacing the concept of migration with that of mobility.

Develop a mutual program aimed at hiring qualified teachers to send to Tunisia, especially in interior areas with the task of providing the youth with more opportunities and, at the same time, hiring Tunisian teachers to assist their peers in European countries, especially those where large numbers of young Tunisians live (Germany, France, Italy). This would have a twofold benefit, reducing unemployment in Europe and Tunisia and having an impact on the educational system in both countries. These teachers would not replace national units, but would support the teaching process, facilitating integration and cultural sharing.

Assist the national government in the deployment of reforms for youth empowerment through access to expert policy makers.

Europe has available a large number of highly skilled professional experts in this field.

The second alternative is where Europe takes on the initiative itself according to its interests, using Tunisian institutions as support. In this regard the most urgent policy would be to recognise the sheer scale of graduates and highly skilled youth

in Tunisia and encourage its member states' companies to plan new strategies of investment in the country. This would match European know-how with the human resources on the ground. The energy sector is the most relevant domain in this regard, especially in the renewable sector. Tunisia's environment presents many opportunities given the large amount of potential green energy from the sun and wind. Several companies in Europe could invest in the high number of young Tunisian engineers. Some things have been done and there are a couple of projects currently operating on the ground, but they are not adequately structured. Other areas which present opportunities for investment are the tourism and food sectors. In doing so Europe has to ensure labour rights, avoiding the exploitation of "cheap labour". Furthermore, European companies should avoid using local labour forces for their own interests in a time-planned period. Instead, they have to foster a process of enrolment in the company's network or encourage workers to gain experience in other projects abroad.

Concluding observations and recommendations for the national government

Tunisia is living through a crucial moment in its history. The country, emerging as an exception in the region, has completed a process of transition to democracy and aims at consolidating its institutions. External and internal pressures from conservative and radical forces have increased their strength across the country, affecting its stability.

Tunisia has demonstrated to the world how young Tunisians' frustration can be channelled into transformative political and social change. It remains to be seen if Tunisia will be able to achieve a more complex goal: stabilising its democracy and consolidating its institutions. Much of this depends on the new generations, mostly those who have actively fuelled the Tunisian transition process since 2010. Youth in Tunisia is a double-edged sword for this process. The cornerstone of their empowerment is their involvement in the system and engagement in its activities. Further exclusion and detachment however could unleash unknown reactions, affecting national stability and jeopardizing what has been achieved thus far.

Consolidation has to focus on groups and their participation within the process. Thus, participation must be found at the "horizontal" level, among political parties and trade and labour unions in order to proceed with a shared and legitimated path within the institutional arena. But, most importantly, participation must be found on the "vertical" plane, among political parties and citizens, especially among young Tunisians who were the soul of the revolution and now are becoming more and more detached, causing scepticism with the promises of the current government. Young Tunisians are the key group to involve, empower and give a voice to within the consolidation process, for the following reasons: they represent the majority of

Tunisia's population;they will be the dominant class of tomorrow; and they were the core of Tunisian revolution.

The National government has to put youth empowerment at the forefront of its agenda. Facilitating youth inclusion will enable the mobilisation of the new generation as an economic and social asset. In this regard strategies that the Tunisian government could adopt are to:

Create a permanent board of specialists and recognised experts, with different backgrounds and fields of expertise. They should be divided into small teams (4-5 units) and deployed regionally, in order to gather youth energy and initiatives. This should be facilitated through the selection of youth leaders at the regional level who would cooperate closely with the teams in supporting the deployment of activities. In an advanced phase, if the feedback is positive and the participation increases, the creation of regional youth councils will be an asset, since a broader and stronger interaction between national representatives and youth would allow leverage to be exerted on the decision making process both at a local and national level. The outcome would be to raise participation and increase the perception of being part of the system, so reducing any feelings of detachment. In order to preserve individual input the national government has to painstakingly select its experts, relying also on independent international organisations which are already involved in empowering youth, in sustaining its activities and cooperating as much as is possible.

Focus on the needs of youths in the interior areas where the level of poverty and detachment is higher, in order to balance inequalities and to pave the way for the creation or the restoration of a middle class. Reducing the gap between the coastal and the interior areas, in terms of opportunities, services and education will be a valuable strategy to avoid new clashes. In this context the deployment of tailored policies, especially in the fields of education and job creation, should be a priority for the government.

Create a more protected environment to support and encourage youth entrepreneurship. Tunisia is a country with a sheer scale of youth entrepreneurial initiatives, with a rising number of small but strong startups.

In this vein, the reduction of barriers and constraints, along with tailored social policy is the main challenge for the national government. It has to guarantee entry into the formal economy with registration and licenses to operate from the government, deterring people from the operation of informal businesses.

There should be a focus on contract enforcement and on the eradication of practices which limit free competition and, in turn, curtail the opportunities and market accessibility for many youth entrepreneurs.

Protecting property rights and the rule of law should be considered, which suffer from major flaws. In this vein, the government should also deploy policies aimed at assisting young entrepreneurs who have been affected by bankruptcy.

Dealing with the rising issue of school dropouts, by intervening with policies to reintroduce students back to school or, as an alternative, orient them towards the job market.

Encourage participation of the youth in social and political activities in order to increase their perception of being a force to build a better country. Participation in social and political activities would restore relations between public authorities and the younger generations. In doing so national government should empower those institutions which are already structured on the ground (trade unions, NGOs, social student unions), by providing them with training, expertise, logistical support and reliable institutional channels.

Transition Torn Between Democratic Consolidation and Neo-Conservatism

The "Arab Spring" of 2011 has not only provoked the fall of different autocratic regimes, new political conflicts and civil wars, and the resurgence of certain "old" conflicts, but it also challenges the debate on democratisation, transition or transformation processes in the countries of North Africa and the Middle East.

Until recently, the theoretical debate mostly concentrated on explaining the absence of transformation, supporting notions of the so-called "Arab exceptionalism" or "Arab resilience" to democratic reforms (Huntington, 1996; Bellin, 2004; Hinnebush, 2006; Pratt 2007). While some analysis considered the chances for democratisation in the Arab world (Anderson, 2006), the majority of the scientific literature concentrated on explaining the mechanisms that authoritarian regimes had developed to stay in power, to endure international pressures and to suppress or co-opt popular dissent (Heydemann, 2007; Ottaway & Choucair-Vizoso, 2008; Gandhi & Lust-Okar, 2009; Cavatorta, 2010). However, the recent popular uprisings, inducing the fall of some of the most resilient and long-lasting regimes in the MENA region (such as the Ben Ali regime in Tunisia, Mubarak regime in Cairo, Gaddafi regime in Libya, and Saleh regime in

Yemen) challenge these theoretical theories, even if in some of these countries counter-revolutions followed the fall of the former regimes. The uprisings of 2011 showed that these regimes were less resilient than thought, and could actually be overthrown within a few days or weeks.

Since the uprisings of 2011 the notions of "transformation" and "transition" are widely employed and often in an indistinct manner. Transformation means "change" or transformation from one political system or regime to another, including profound political, economic, social and cultural changes within the society. Transformation does not automatically mean a regime change towards democracy and pluralism (Merkel, 2010).The notion of "transition" is often put equal on terms with "transition to democracy" (O'Donnell et al., 1986), even though the authors distanced themselves from a normative understanding of implied democratisation.In this paper, "transition" is understood in a comprehensive manner, as a process of change with an open end. The notion of transition has a more dynamic character than transformation; transformation happens over years and decades; a transition from one regime or government to a new system can happen in a few days, as the Tunisian example has shown, even if the administrative body or security sector for instance were not carried along by the transition dynamic. With regard to the political class, one can even speak of a kind of neo-conservative turn, in the sense of a potential comeback of ancient regime structures and networks. Reforms can generate political, economic, cultural or social change, transition or transformation. They can bring forward pluralism, political participation or the respect for fundamental rights and freedoms. The theoretical "democratisation debate" should be revised in the light of the "Arab Spring" and its aftermath, but this is not the intention of this paper, which focuses instead on the current and on-going transition process in Tunisia. The Tunisian transition consists of different contradictory, multifaceted dynamics and movements that might tear the society apart, or create an even stronger resilience towards external radicalised pressures.

The newly emerging Tunisian political system needs to be considered in the context of the current developments in the wider MENA region. In the international political and scientific debate on the "Arab Spring", the Tunisian case has often been cited as a "model" of peaceful and successful transition. This paper rather considers the Tunisian transition as a very particular and unique case, and not as a "model". Compared to other (failing or not failing) states in the MENA region, it is indeed the only country where a comprehensive process of democratic consolidation is taking place so far. The hitherto success of the Tunisian transition results from the particular constellation of the Tunisian case, including the constructive combination of different factors such as a strong civil society, strong middle class, low level of armament, consensus-oriented tradition, high level of education, or the absence of violent ethnic conflicts. All these factors suggest that the perspectives for a long-term democratic transformation process look positive but the challenges remain multifaceted. The paper assesses the different phases and achievements of the transition process (in section 1), before looking at the challenges, difficulties and future perspectives.

Major Phases and Achievements in the Tunisian Transition Process

Tunisia has achieved major milestones on its way to establishing a democratic system. Amongst these milestones are the building of the three reform commissions right after the Tunisian revolution in 2011, the foundation of a new political party landscape, the first free elections in October 2011 (after 23 years of the Ben Ali regime), building the legitimate basis for the National Constituent Assembly (NCA) in November 2011, the adoption of the new constitution in January 2014, and last but not least the first free legislative elections (October 2014) and presidential elections (November/December 2014). The abolition of the emergency law in March 2014 was a further milestone.The role of the civil society has been very important throughout the whole process. All these milestones have come about in a peaceful context. There have been some incidents of political violence though (especially in 2013), and two brutal terrorist attacks (Bardo, Sousse/El-Kantaoui 2015), but compared to the developments in other countries of the region, especially in Libya or Syria, the political transition in Tunisia has been relatively calm, non-violent and participative (although about 338 people died during the revolution, and about 2,200 people were injured).

After the Revolution Building Reform Commissions

After the Tunisian revolution and the fall of the Ben Ali regime on 14 January 2011, a new and unknown political and social dynamic spread in the country. The number of newly created civil society organisations and new political parties exploded. More than 100 political parties were founded and legalised. The same was true for the media sector. The number of new magazines, newspapers and TV channels rapidly augmented; freedom of the press increased tremendously, and the media sector became more critical, independent and free. Right after the revolution, the official governmental functions were transmitted to interim Prime Minister Mohamed Ghanoucci, and to interim President of the Parliament Fouad Mebazaâ. This transition government (in office from 17 January 2011 to 27 February 2011) announced as one of the first steps to guarantee a comprehensive freedom of the press and information, and the release of all political prisoners (about 500).But due to political tensions and protests, another transition government took office (27 February-13 December 2011) under Béji Caid Essebsi, who was the last transition Prime Minister before the elections of October 2011.

Alongside the transition governments, three reform commissions were set up in 2011, with the task to politically and institutionally prepare the ground for the first free elections

of the National Constituent Assembly (NCA). Step by step, the electoral law was changed, and the preparations for the elections started. In particular, Yadh Ben Achour played an important and constructive role in this critical and fragile phase by leading the Haute Commission nationale pour la réforme politique (Higher Political Reform Commission of Tunisia), which became a sort of transitional parliament, by calming down heated debates and political conflicts. The Commission nationale d'établissement des faits sur les affaires de malversations et de corruption was chaired by Abdelfattah Amor, and the Commission nationale des faits sur les abus durant la dernière période by Taoufik Bouderbala.

Major challenges in this first transition phase were: the social pacification of the society, the credibility of the new institutions and new political leaders, the continued presence of foreign enterprises and investments, and the return of tourism. The expectations of the society were very high: after the fall of the old regime everything should change for the better from one day to another. Right after the revolution, most of the "revolutionaries" expected and hoped for a sudden improvement of their daily life and material situation, a new job, a decrease in food prices. Many citizens were hoping for more justice too, and a punishment of former plaguers. At this point of time, people demonstrated for so long, until no more members of the former single party Rassemblement constitutionnel démocratique (RCD) or members of former governments (under Ben Ali) would be part of one of the transition governments.Anger and disrespect were strong, and tolerance toward former regime members and collaborators was very limited. This attitude changed later on, along with the slowly growing disappointment with the lack of tangible results of the revolution.

A New Political Party Landscape

Since January 2011, the emerging political party landscape has been very dynamic. About 107 new political parties were accredited after the revolution; eight already existed before.Different party coalitions and alliances were built, split up again, reconfigured, and changed their names, objectives and strategies a number of times. The pluralisation of the political party landscape is definitely a democratic milestone of the Tunisian transition process, compared to the (almost) single party system before, with the RCD as the only party capable of acting. A formal party pluralism had existed since 1988, but in reality under the "ancient regime", only a few pseudo opposition parties were allowed (e.g. Parti de l'unité populaire [PUP], Union démocratique unioniste [UDU], Mouvement des democrats socialistes [MDS]). In addition, a few real opposition parties (e.g. Ettajdid, Forum Démocratique pour le Travail et les Libertés [FDTL], Parti Démocrate Progressiste [PDP]) existed, but were facing repression. None of the existing parties at the time could have won any elections.

In a first phase after the revolution, there was a tendency of great fragmentation into numerous small parties and alliances.

In January 2011 all political parties forbidden until then were legalised. In a second phase, some smaller parties disappeared or joined other parties, and some political forces became more evident and visible. In 2015, the party landscape includes parties of a great ideological spectrum, from far left to far right as well as religious parties. These major currently existing political forces are described below.

Major political factions

Neo-conservative parties

The new central political party in this faction is Nidaa Tounes, founded in 2012 by Béji Caid Essebsi, is a neo-conservative party and defines itself as a political movement in the tradition of Habib Bourguiba, close to the Doustour movement. Party Leader Essebsi was already active in politics under presidents Bourguiba and Ben Ali (during the first years of the regime). It brings together a great mixture of people, whose main common ground is the interest to weaken the Islamist movement, to return to law and order; it addresses the concerns of the liberal middle class. The party can mobilise the local networks of former RCD members and followers. Under its umbrella, former regime representatives and followers gather together with economic liberals, some trade unionists (e.g. Tayyeb Baccouche) and intellectuals (e.g. lawyer and women's activist Bochra Ben Hamida). The success of Nidaa Tounes can be explained by the wish of the majority of the population for more stability and security after agitated phases in 2013, but also by the negative experiences that had been made with the Ennahda-led Troika government (2012-2013). In 2014, even some leftist and liberals called to vote utile for Nidaa Tounes – all united against Ennahda. Finally, this strategy worked for the party, which became the major political force and won the legislative and presidential elections in 2014. The Initiative nationale destourienne (Al Moubarada) (National Destourian Initiative) defines itself as a centrist political party. It was founded in 2011, but came out of the former RCD party. The party leader is Kamel Morjane, former Minister of Defence and Foreign Affairs under Ben Ali. The party merged with different smaller parties in 2014, and won 3 seats in the new parliament.

Islamist parties

Right after the revolution, the Ennahda party (or Ennahda Movement), founded in 1981 but officially forbidden under the Ben Ali regime, was one of the first political parties to receive an official accreditation in March 2011. The objective of Ennahda is the Islamisation of Tunisian society and of the political system, the promotion of Islamic values, and the implementation of the Sharia in a mid- or long-term perspective. The party's strategy is tactical and pragmatic, and ready to compromise. Ennahda is well organised, and has a large network of members and followers throughout the country. The network of mosques is used as an efficient tool of mobilisation of large parts of the population in all regions of the country. In addition, the party receives financial and political support from Ennahda members living abroad (e.g. Great Britain, France) and from like-minded Gulf countries (especially Qatar). The success of Ennahda is explained by its credibility as opposition movement to the former regime.Ennahda also presents itself as the party of the excluded and disinherited. Ennahda politicians speak the language of the common people, another factor explaining its popularity. However, the party was also accused of buying votes through the distribution of money and presents, at in the different elections. Internally, the party consists of different wings, including ideological hardliners and power- oriented pragmatics. The latter wing is considered to be "moderate", pragmatic and "Islam-Democrat" oriented (e.g. Hamadi Jebali, although his discourse became harder after the Ennahda coalition with Nidaa Tounes), and represents about one third of the party members. The ideological hardliner wing is ready to use violence and brutal methods in order to achieve its political goals. A third wing is ideologically and politically close to the Salafist movement, more present within the party base, and represented by politicians like Habib Ellouz or Sadok Chourou. The Choura Council represents an internal party forum for debating and deciding the party's positions and strategies. Party leader Rashid al Ghanoushi tries to keep control over the different currents. The electoral campaigns changed from religious and national identity issues in 2011 toward more socioeconomic issues in 2014. The party base was and still is upset about the coalition with Nidaa Tounes.

Next to Ennahda, the Salafist movement is also part of the Islamist political spectrum. At the moment of the revolution, the Salafist movement was rather small (about 200 members). In the aftermath, the movement became stronger and arranged an agreement with Ennahda, including Salafist support for Ennahda during the first elections in 2011. The ultra-conservative Salafist movement is ideologically close to and supported by Wahhabite foundations from Saudi Arabia. The objective is the creation of an Islamic State and the imposition of Islamic law (Sharia). The Salafist movement is divided into a reformist current (ready to participate in the parliamentary system) and a radical Jihadist current. Salafist parties, however, did not take part in the elections for the NCA in 2011. The first Salafist party in Tunisia, Hizb-ut-Tahrir (Party of Liberation), did not receive a party accreditation for the 2011 elections, but was legalised in July 2012. However, this party still rejects democratic rules and elections as a tool of alternation. It calls for the Caliphate, uses the same flag as the Islamic State (IS), and plans to install the centre of the Caliphate in North Africa. After the terrorist attack in Sousse 2015 by a radical Islamist, the party came under stronger political pressure and might be forbidden by the authorities. Observers fear that the party members will go underground then and further radicalise. Three Salafist parties were created and officialised afterwards: The Front de la réforme, Jabhat Al Islah (Islah Front), under Mohammed Khoja, was officialised in 2012, and claims to respect democracy and the civic nature of the state.The party's objective is to encourage observance of Islamic values, but by democratic means. The Parti de l'authenticité (Hizb Al Asala) is led by Mouldi Moujahed; the Parti de la miséricorde (Hizb Arrahma) was legalised in July 2012 and is led by Said Al Jaziri.

Shifting from the Secular Left towards the Islamist faction?

The Congrès pour la République (Congress for the Republic, CPR) is a centre republican party, founded in 2001 by Moncef Marzouki, forbidden under the Ben Ali regime, and re- legalised in March 2011. The ideological orientation is Arab-national. But the party also brought together a large number of dissidents from Nahda living abroad (e.g. Lotfi Zeitoun, Slim Ben H'Miden, Imed Daimi – current secretary general of the CPR). Party leader Marzouki, a former human rights activist of the Ligue Tunisienne des Droits de l'Homme (LTDH), became the first president of the new Tunisia in December 2011; he was designated after a long dealing process between Ettakatol, Nahda and the CPR. The CPR participated in the first Troika government (2012-2013), but lost many members, ministers, MPs and followers, mainly because of its coalition and rapprochement with the Islamist party Ennahda, but also because of internal conflicts. The secretary general left the party in the ANC period, as well as 17 of 29 members who joined other parties or founded new parties (e.g. Wafa). The exercise of political responsibility in the government, in the NCA, and the performance of the Presidency actually weakened the party. Initially founded as an opposition party to the ancient regime, the major party objective was the overthrow of the Ben Ali regime; today the party's objectives are, among others, an anti-neoliberal economic policy and opposition toward the IMF's and World Bank plans for Tunisia. Marzouki experienced increasing unpopularity and progressively approached Ennahda. After his failure in the presidential elections 2014, he founded a new Mouvance du peuple des citoyens.

Secular Left

The Front Populaire (Popular Front), founded in 2012, is an extreme leftist party, and brings together 12 small parties, most of them former communist parties: Marxists, Arab nationalists, and left extremists, although most of them avoid strong militancy. The party leader is Hamma Hammami, a popular communist, already active in the opposition under the Ben Ali regime. The assassinated opposition politician Chokri Belaid was an important member, and especially efficient in bringing the different ideological groups together. Members and followers are mainly workers and intellectuals. The second opposition politician Mohamed Brahmi, founder of the People's Movement, assassinated in July 2013, was temporarily an important member of the Front Populaire (in 2013) and a member of the NCA. A further party member, Mohamed Belmufti, died during a solidarity demonstration for Mohamed Brahmi in July 2013 (killed by tear gas). The death of these respected politicians actually led to a rise in the popularity of the party, too, and a greater electoral success in 2014 than in 2011. The Mouvement du peuple (People's Movement) was legalised in 2011 and is a socialist, secularist, and Arab nationalist party. It was temporarily a member of the Front Populaire (see above), and split up and merged different times. The former leader, Mohamed Brahmi, was assassinated in 2013. The party stands for "freedom, socialism and unity", and is close to workers' groups.

Ettakatol is a social-democrat party, founded in 1994 by Mustafa Ben Jaafar, who became the president of the NCA in 2011.His party was one of the rare and real opposition parties (Forum démocratique pour le travail et les libertés [FDTL]) existing under the Ben Ali regime, and represents an alternative to the traditional left. The party struggles for social equality and socially just economic growth. The party also lost many members, ministers, NCA members and followers because of its participation in the Troika coalition government with Ennahda (10 of 20 NCA members left the party). Ben Jaafar was in favour of a strategic dialogue with Ennahda and its inclusion in the new political party system, for avoiding its political marginalisation and potential radicalisation. For strategic reasons he also cooperated more closely with Nahda than with the CPR, and was ready to accept the first version of the constitutional draft, largely dominated by Nahda proposals. However, in the end, thanks to his integrative and inclusive approach, he played a central role in bringing together the different political factions within the NCA, and in succeeding with the final adoption of the new constitution.

Afek Tounes (Tunisian Aspiration), founded in 2011, stands for a liberal economic and societal programme. The party leader is Yassine Brahim. The party won 4 seats in the NCA, and 8 seats in the new Assembly of the Representatives of the People (ARP). It represents itself as a modern, secular, westernised minority party, centre-conservative- liberal, and as a young political force. Its programme includes detailed plans for a fiscal reform.

Further objectives are the support of individual entrepreneurship, the creation of new jobs, and the defence of fundamental rights. Members and followers come from the liberal upper and middle class and the intellectual elites. After a relatively small electoral success in 2011, Afek Tounes founded in April 2012 a party alliance – the new "Republican Party" – together with the former Parti Démocrate Progressiste (PDP) of Nahijb Chebbi, Al Joumhouri (the Tunisian Republican Party) and other centre and social- liberal parties. The objective of this party alliance was to build a democratic force of the middle class and the political centre. But the party alliance broke apart again in August 2013. Afek Tounes continued on its own, and the Tunisian Republican Party continued under its old name Al Joumhouri (Republican Party). The Party defines itself as the continuity of the former PDP, and stands for social liberalism, liberalism, social democracy and progress. The current party leader is Maya Jribi, but Nejib Chebbi is still part of the leadership.

Al Massar (the Democratic and Social Voice), founded in 2012, is the result of a fusion of the former Ettajdid Movement, the Tunisian Work Party (PTT) and independents from the former Modernist Democratic Pole (PDM). In the NCA, al Massar held 5 seats, then 10, because of the following affiliation of five other NCA representatives. Al Massar also became a member of the alliance Union for Tunisia. It represents a centre-left political party of and for the elites, including many university teachers, professors, intellectuals and artists.

Courant Démocratique, Attayar (Democratic Current) was founded in 2013; the current leader is Mohamed Abbou, a former deputy minister in charge of public administration reform and governance in the Hamadi Jebali government, who left the CPR. The political orientation of the party is pan-

Arabism. However, it maintains a close relationship with the CPR and Nahda. Currently, Attayar is part of Moncef Marzouki's recent initiative called Hirak Chaab al Mouatinoun (People of Citizen's Movement). The party's objective is the creation of an Arab federal state, uniting the Arab states, freed from dictatorship. The party won 3 seats in the new parliament.

New Populists

The Union Patriotique Libre (Free Patriotic Union, UPL), founded in 2011 by the populist entrepreneur Slim Riahi, won 2 seats in the NCA, and was rather successful in the legislative elections of 2014 (with 16 seats it is the third strongest party in the new parliament). The party is extremely populist, for example in terms of anti-terrorism combat, and has the objective to facilitate investment conditions for large economic projects. Party leader Riahi made his fortune in Libya where his parents lived in exile during the times of the Ben Ali regime. He maintained close relations with Gaddafi's son Saif al- Islam. Tayyar al-Mahabba (Current of Love), founded in 2013, came out of the former Al Aridha Chaabia Party, also called Petition populaire pour la Liberté, la Justice et le Développement (Popular Petition), founded in 2011 by the entrepreneur Mohamed Hechmi Hamdi. Hamdi lives in Great Britain, campaigns for the socioeconomic development of Tunisia, and is politically close to Ennahda. He is also the founder of the Arab television channel Al Mustaquilla, based in London; his discourse is rather populist. His party had a surprising electoral success during the elections for the National Constituent Assembly in 2011 (26 seats). Given the fact that the party leader is not very present in Tunisia, that there is no real political party structure, and that the party members have rather different agendas, the party lost a lot of voices in the elections of 2014 and won only 2 seats.

Current opposition parties

Among the opposition parties, which are not represented in the current parliament, there are: the Democratic Forum for Labour and Liberties (Ettakatol), Destourian Movement, Justice and Development Party, Maghrebi Republican Party, Pirate Party, Popular Unity Movement, Popular Unity Party, Reform Front Party, Social Democratic Path, Social Liberal Party, Tunisian Pirate Party, Unionist Democratic Union, Voice of the People of Tunisia, Wafa Movement, and Al-Watan Party.

The new multiparty system continues to be fluid and in motion, but represents the major important political and historical currents of Tunisia: liberal reformism, Islam, and the left, as well as secondary currents such as pan-Arab nationalism and Baathism, liberal nationalism in the tradition of Bourguiba, communism, Marxism, and ecology (M'Rad, 2014, pp. 151-153). The wide spectrum of new and old political parties illustrates the significant pluralisation and fragmentation of political currents, political personnel and leadership that took place after the fall of the Ben Ali regime.

Elections of the National Constituent Assembly (NCA) in October 2011

The elections for the National Constituent Assembly took place on 23 October 2011 in a free and fair manner. The number of political parties had decreased by then, and only 77 of 115 decided to take part in the elections.Organised by the Independent Election Committee (ISIE), under the responsibility of human rights activist Kamel Jendoubi, the results of the elections surprised in different terms: the first surprise was the overwhelming success of the Islamist party Ennahda with about 41% of the seats, and 89 seats out of 217 in the National Constituent Assembly (NCA), which corresponds to 37% of the total number of votes.The second surprise was the low turnout of voters with about 51.7% of the registered voters. Among the 7,569,824 of voting age only 4,123,602 were registered to vote, and only 3,702,627 actually voted on 23 October. Finally, the electoral success of Moncef Marzouki's CPR and Hechmi Hamdi's Al Aridha Party were not expected in the run- up to the elections. The ANC was initially elected for one year and had the ambitious plan to finish the drafting of a new constitution within one year. Finally, the NCA continued to function, alongside its task of constitution drafting, as a de facto transitional parliament until the end of 2014, when the first new parliament and a new President of the Second Republic were elected. The NCA officially met for the first time on 22 November 2011. Moncef Marzouki was elected by the NCA as Interim President on 12 December 2011, and stayed in office until the end of 2014.

Members of the ANC (217 seats) in 2011

Political Party	Number of Seats
Ennahda	89
Congrès pour la République (CPR)	29
Al Aridha/Petition populaire	26
Ettakatol	20
Parti démocrate progressiste (PDP)	16
Independents	8
Pôle démocratique moderniste (PDM)	5
L'Initiative (former RCD, Hizb Al Moubarada)	5

Afek Tounes	4
Parti communiste des ouvriers de Tunisie (PCOT)	3
Al Badil Al Thawri	3
Mouvement du peuple/Courant populaire	2
Mouvement des démocrates socialistes	2
Union patriotique libre (UPL)	1
Parti unifié des patriotes democrats	1
Parti républicain maghrébin	1
Parti de la nation culturel et unioniste	1
Parti de la lutte progressiste	1
Parti démocrate-social de la nation	1
Parti du Néo-Destour	1
Parti de l'èquité et de l'égalité	1
Total number	217
Voter turnout	51.7%

At the end of the NCA's working period in 2014, the configuration and party distribution of the NCA looked very different. Some parties disappeared, some were newly created, and some NCA members left their parties and joined others.

The representation of women in the new institutions has increased since 2011.In the NCA, about 27% of the members were female representatives. Among the 49 NCA female members, 42 were Ennahda party members, and 7 women members represented the leftist, secular wing. The Vice-President of the NCA was a woman: the French-Tunisian Ennahda member Merhezia Labidi-Maiza (constituency Paris 1).

Succeeding Governments, Political Crises, Reform Process (December 2011-January 2014)

As a result of the NCA elections a first coalition government was formed in December 2011. The so-called Troika government included Ennahda, the Congrès pour la République (CPR) and Ettakatol. President Marzouki officially appointed Hamadi Jebali (Ennahda) as Prime Minister on 24 December 2011. Given the fact that Ennahda was the majority party at this point in time, most of the key ministries were given to Ennahda members (except the Ministry of Defence). Both coalition parties (CPR and Ettakatol) lost a lot of party members and followers because of their coalition with Ennahda; this coalition option had not been explicitly communicated during their electoral campaigns. In particular, many young members and followers of Ettakatol were disappointed with this decision. They had fought during the revolution for more freedom, rights, social equality and professional perspectives, and felt betrayed by the party leadership, being too indulgent in their eyes of Ennahda politicians and their political objectives. The leftist and smaller progressive parties, many of them united under the umbrella of the Pôle démocratique moderniste (Democratic Modernist Pole, PDM), did not have the electoral success they had expected. Many were shocked by the success of Ennahda.

The first ruling period of Ennahda was finally rather short (December 2011-January 2014).However, during this time period Ennahda tried to hinder reforms instead of pushing them forward, for instance in the justice and security sector. The party occupied major positions at important locations in the administration, media, education system and other sectors with its own people, according to political party-related criteria, and not according to competence. Within the Ministry of the Interior and the Ministry of Social Affairs responsible officers were replaced, and in local administrations new Ennahda governors were nominated. In May 2012, for instance, 82 judges were replaced without any justification (Bauchard, 2013, p. 6). A Ministry of Transitional Justice and Human Rights was newly created and appointed to Samir Dilou (Ennahda); but the government was actually accused of continuity of repression. Only the Ministry of Foreign Affairs stayed more or less as it was, and was not touched by Ennahda's personnel policy. The Ennahda-led Troika government was also criticised for being too indulgent with radical actions of ultra-conservative Salafists, while confrontations between other demonstrators and the police often ended with brutal repression from the police side. Further critical attacks targeted the government's lack of efficient decision-making in terms of important economic and financial reforms, and of good governance. The Ennahda government was criticised for "sustainable deformation by a religiously oriented pseudo-democratic societal model" (Braune, 2012) and, last but not least, accused of corruption and cronyism. All these factors resulted in a phase of stagnation and blockade of the political and economic decision-making process. On the other hand, parts of the Ennahda party showed increasing willingness to negotiate and to compromise with its governmental coalition partners, and later on in the process of constitution-making (see 1.5.).

In the course of 2012 and 2013, a certain polarisation between an Islamist majority and the liberal secular opposition grew within the NCA and within the wider Tunisian society. Among the liberal opposition, one can distinguish a regrouping around two poles: a centre- republican pole and a leftist-liberal pole. After the assassination of Chokri Belaid on 6 February 2013, belonging to the leftist-liberal pole, and a well-known public critic of Ennahda, Ennahda came under increasing political pressure. Prime Minister Hamadi Jebali proposed to establish a new "technocrat government".In addition, a Conseil des sages was built, including about 16 personalities, with an average age of 80+, supporting the Islamist movement, but also some representatives of important Tunisian families, such as Ahmed Mestiri and Yadh Ben Achour, as well as General Rachid Ammar as an observer (Bauchard, 2013, p. 10). Until this moment, Hamadi Jebali as head of government and Rashid Ghanoushii as head of the Ennahda party successfully shared their tasks. But Ghanoucci and the Conseil de la Choura did not support the idea of a "technocrat government", and wanted to keep the control of power and the key ministries exclusively for Ennahda. Hamadi Jebali resigned on 19 February 2013 after his proposal was not implemented. Finally, Ali Larayedh (former Minister of the Interior, Ennahda) formed a new government in February/March 2013, a mixture of external experts and party members, which was considered as a concession by Ennahda and Ghanoucci towards the opposition. But the secular opposition remained very sceptical and mistrustful towards Ennahda. The political crisis became even stronger in 2013 (after the assassination of Mohamed Brahmi in July 2013 and the protest of 60 NCA opposition members), so that at the beginning of 2014, and after the mediation efforts of the "National Dialogue", Ennahda voluntarily withdrew from power, and a "technocrat government" under Mehdi Jomaa (former Minister of Industry, impartial) was officially appointed on 29 January 2014. The Jomaa government remained in power for about one year (until 31 December 2014).

Besides these political crises and increasing economic difficulties, the different governments were constantly criticised for not dissolving the so-called "Leagues of the Revolution". These leagues were spontaneously created during the revolution, but more systematically after the revolution, with the support of Ennahda, which used them for controlling the population; in 2013, there were still about 80 leagues.The leagues use arbitrary violence in order to threaten and frighten the population, on the pretext of securing the objectives of the revolution. The dissolution of the leagues was demanded by the civil society several times, and promised by several politicians, including Hamadi Jebali, but not implemented.

At the same time, in this phase between 2011 and 2014, and despite the aforementioned difficulties and crises, a certain number of political reforms have been implemented and political freedoms generally increased. In addition, reforms in the fields of justice, education, the economy and fiscal law have been implemented since 2011. New legal and financial frameworks have been established for the new administrations and bodies, especially in the fields of audio-visual communication, supervision of justice, combating corruption, anti-torture measures, external control of public funds, and transitional justice.And despite the difficult political context in 2013, important measures in relation to rule of law and fundamental rights were adopted. These measures include:

- ❧ The establishment of an Instance nationale de prévention de la torture et d'autres peines ou traitements cruels, inhumains et dégradants (National Association of Torture Prevention) in October 2013 by the National Constituent Assembly. This measure is part of the obligations of the Protocole facultatif der Convention contre la torture et autres traitements cruels, inhumains et dégradants, which was signed by Tunisia in June 2011 (60th state that signed).

&. A new law on the establishment of an Instance provisoire pour la supervision de la justice judiciaire Preliminary (Committee for the Supervision of Judiciary Justice, IPSJJ). This instance is supposed to contribute to strengthening the independence of the judiciary.

&. The Instance nationale de lutte contre la corruption (National Association Against Corruption) could no longer work in 2013, and was replaced by the Conseil supérieur de lutte contre la corruption.

&. In August 2013, the Tunisian government classified the radical-Islamist group Ansar Al-Sharia as a "terrorist organisation". This was an important step towards a clear demarcation by Ennahda from radical groups within the broader Islamist movement. Further small reforms were implemented in the fields of evaluation of fiscal policy, rationalisation of control of public funds, as well as in the modernisation of public accounting systems.

These kinds of reform steps encouraged international donors to continue supporting the Tunisian transition. For instance, in 2014 the EU defined, in cooperation with the Tunisian negotiation delegation, the following priorities in the new ENP Action Plan for the upcoming years: guarantee of human rights and freedom of press and of expression; guarantee of respect of women's rights; implementation of torture prevention mechanisms; implementation of the mobility partnership; reform of the security sector; additional reforms in favour of an independent judiciary, economic reforms and reforms of public funding.Besides the EU, numerous other external actors and donor programmes have supported Tunisia even more intensively since 2011.

Despite the aforementioned political difficulties, further domestic and regional ups and downs, the constitutional activities of the NCA continued step by step. And despite very difficult and long debate processes within the NCA, on every single article, the constitutional process went on, and came to a constructive and inclusive result with the adoption of the new constitution in January 2014.

Adoption of the New Constitution in January 2014

One of the most important milestones of the Tunisian transition process certainly was the adoption of the new constitution on 27 January 2014, combining a civic state with Islam as state religion.200 of 216 NCA members voted in favour of the constitution (12 against, 4 abstentions), which guarantees fundamental rights and freedoms, human rights, freedom of faith, gender equality, and introduces new rights, such as the right to a proper environment. The Sharia is not mentioned in the constitutional text, and does not represent a source of law. The constitution was officially and solemnly celebrated in the NCA on 7 February 2014.

The constitution is the result of a long process of controversial debate about the character of the new political system and the societal order. Different views between the moderate-Islamist Ennahda parliamentary group and the different liberal-secular oriented factions rendered the decision-making process arduous. Contentious issues included: the civil character of the state, the importance attributed to the Islamic religion in the constitution, the conditions of a vote of no confidence, and the guarantee of the political impartiality of educational institutions.In the beginning of the constitutional process,

Ennahda asked for the Sharia to be mentioned in the constitutional text, and defined women and men as "complementary" and not as "equal". After the deterrent developments in Egypt where the Muslim Brothers despite and after their electoral success and the transitory Mursi Presidency were declared a "terrorist organisation" in 2013, Ennahda changed its political strategy and became more open to political compromise. Finally, the Sharia is not mentioned as a source of law, and the constitution became a sort of compromise between a secular and religious oriented society model. Actually, the article on freedom of faith (Art. 6) is progressive in comparison to many other constitutions, while Art. 21 guarantees gender equality before the law. However, Art. 7 defines the family as the "nucleus of society and the state shall protect it", and thereby opens up possibilities of interpretation in favour of male family patriarchs (e.g. in the domain of adoption and divorce law).On the other hand, the progressive Art. 46 provides important "women's rights" in terms of equal representation. The categorisation of a polarisation process between a secular and a religious faction within the political spectrum (and within the wider society), does not however take into account that the lines between these two poles are very fluid. For instance, different Ennahda NCA members have also pleaded for more freedom rights. In sum, the compromise on the constitution can be considered as a historical, progressive and symbolic achievement for all involved political factions, as well as for the Tunisian political transition process.

In the new political system of the 2nd Republic, the role of the President of the Republic is reduced, due to the negative experiences with the former presidential system, instrumentalised by Ben Ali. While Ben Ali saw himself above the constitution, he also used it as a tool for extending state power and directing the institutions of state in his favour (Pickard,

2014, p. 136). The new constitution strengthens the role of the Prime Minister and of the Parliament: the Assembly of the Representatives of the People (ARP). The objective is to share the executive power between the President and the Prime Minister in order to avoid a potential autocratic consolidation of power. The number of presidential terms is limited to two (five years each). A new Constitutional Court – responsible for controlling the constitutional right of future legislative reforms and protecting the separation of powers – will be established. This new court, replacing the former Constitutional Council, is meant to be an equal player to the executive and legislature (Pickard, 2014, p. 137).

However, even if the political system has a stronger Parliament and Prime Minister as before, the power balance of the dual executive (President, Prime Minister) will depend on the political personalities holding these offices. As one can already observe with the presidential mandate of Beji Caid Essebsi (Nidaa Tounes) that the presidential power actually overshadows the role and competences of Prime Minister Habib Essid (Nidaa Tounes).

In January 2014, the NCA also appointed the nine members of the Instance supérieure indépendante pour les elections (Independent Election Committee, ISIE), after a long debate on procedures and potential members. ISIE was charged with preparing the legislative and presidential elections before the end of 2014, in a very brief time period.

Legislative Elections in October 2014

The new parliament, elected on 26 October 2014, called the "Assembly of the Representatives of the People" (ARP) is a unicameral assembly with 217 seats. On 2 December 2014, the new parliament met for the first time. The guidance of the inaugural session was the task of the oldest MPs (Ali Ben Salem, Nidaa Tounes) and the two youngest MPs (Amel Souid, Ennahda) and Chekib Bani (Nidaa Tounes). The former NCA President Mustafa Ben Jaafar (Ettakatol) handed over responsibility to the new President of the Parliament, Mohamed Ennaceur (Nidaa Tounes), after he was elected by the Assembly; two Vice Presidents were appointed: Abdelfattah Mourou (Ennahda) and Faouzia Ben Fodha (UPL).Besides the election of the President of the Parliament, during this inaugural session, a transition committee was elected for the management of the parliament and the public budget, which was in charge until the end of the second round of the presidential elections. The task of this transition committee was mainly to prepare two urgent laws: the new financial law for 2015 and a new anti-terrorism law.

The legislative elections took place between 24 and 26 October 2014, in about 11,000 voting offices. The fear of terrorist attacks was high; therefore the presence of police and army was considerably increased during the election period. The electoral participation was about 69%. The majority of the younger generation did not vote. Voting participation was higher in the coastal regions and in the north, and less in the poorer regions in the centre and the south. International election observers (including an EU electoral observer commission) called the elections "free and fair".

In the new parliament, the distribution of the political parties looks very different in comparison to the NCA elected in 2011:

Members of the ARP in 2014 (217 seats):

Political Party	Number of Seats

Nidaa Tounes	86
Ennahda	69
Free Patriotic Union/Union patriotique libre (UPL)	16

Popular Front/Front Populaire	15
Afek Tounes	8
Congress for the Republic/Congrès pour la République (CPR)	4
Democratic Current	3
People's Movement	3
National Destourian Initiative	3
Current of Love	2
Republican Party (Al Joumhouri)	1
Democratic Alliance	1
Farmers' Voice Party	1
Movement of Socialist Democrats (MDS)	1
National Front for Salvation	1
Independent lists:	
List of the Call of Tunisians Abroad	1
List of the Glory of the Djerid	1
List of Rehabilitation	1

| Total number | 217 |
| Voter turnout | 69% |

The clear winner of the election was Nidaa Tounes. Ennahda lost 20 seats but remains the second strongest political force. Different parties lost a significant number of seats, such as Ettakatol, CPR and the Republican Party compared to the NCA. Ettakatol lost many votes in because of its coalition with Ennahda in the Troika government. Many Ettakatol voters and followers rejected the cooperation with the Islamist faction, and felt disappointed with this decision. In addition, as the smallest coalition partner of the Troika government, Ettakatol worked itself into the ground between Ennadha and the CPR. But the party also did not succeed in mobilising enough critical mass of young members and voters due to the internal party organisation that was not adapted fast enough to the new political situation after the Tunisian revolution, and the lack of focusing political communication on youth and its concerns. Finally, the integrative role played by Ettakatol in the constitutional process was not honoured by the voters.

The CPR fared so poorly because of the increased unpopularity of Moncef Marzouki, who failed to bring about important future-oriented economic and political reforms and visions for Tunisia, and who was neither able to appease the political polarisation within the political and social landscape, nor to appease the security situation. Many former voters were disappointed by his performance as the first president of the new Tunisia.

Building the government required an absolute majority of 109 seats. Therefore, Nidaa Tounes had the right to start coalition negotiations. Before the elections, a coalition between Nidaa Tounes and Ennahda seemed probable (for pragmatic reasons), although the main common denominator between the different internal wings and groups of Nidaa Tounes was the objective to hinder a second overwhelming electoral victory for Ennahda. But then, after the elections, the Nidaa Tounes leadership decided to marginalise Ennahda, and looked for other coalition partners. Finally, Ennahda was integrated into the first new government of the 2nd Republic, but received only one ministry (Employment). One of the reasons was the fear that non-integration of Ennahda might provoke potentially violent protests and anti-governmental mobilisation from the population and Ennahda voters and followers. Further coalition partners are UPL and Afek Tounes. In the ARP, the role of the smaller opposition parties remains difficult and challenging at the same time, as they are facing two major blocks (Nidaa Tounes, Ennahda).

Presidential Elections in November/December 2014 – The End of the Transition Process– The Beginning of the 2nd Republic

According to the new constitution (Art. 75), the President is elected for a five-year term by means of universal, free, direct, secret, fair, and transparent elections, by an absolute majority of votes cast. In the event that no candidate achieves such a majority in the first round, a second round is organised. Only the two candidates having won the highest number of votes during the first round can stand for election in the second round.In order to be able to run for the presidential elections, a minimum of 10,000 supporters' signatures across the country was necessary, or of 10 NCA members. The electoral campaign had started after the legislative elections, and was criticised as a new kind of mud-throwing contest between the candidates, of a "quality" unknown in Tunisia so far. Ennahda and Nidaa Tounes expressed publicly the possibility of a common coalition.

Ennahda decided to not present its own candidate for the presidential elections, in order to counter the accusation of a potential total power accumulation. Until the very last moment, the Ennahda leadership did not clearly take position for Marzouki, and did not explicitly call its members and followers to vote for Marzouki, although many Ennahda members publicly supported Marzouki's candidature.

The first round of the presidential elections took place on 23 November 2014. Finally, 23 candidates were officially allowed to run for office, among them Beji Caid Essebsi (Nidaa Tounes), Moncef Marzouki (CPR), Mustapha Ben Jaafar (Ettakatol), but also Néjib Chebbi (Al Joumhouri), Hamma Hamami (Popular Front), Slim Riahi (UPL) or Hechmi Hamdi (Courant Al Mahabba). The judge Kalthoum Kanou was the only female candidate. In the first round no candidate achieved the absolute majority. The two candidates with the majority of votes were Beji Caid Essebsi (42-47.8%) and Moncef Marzouki (26.9-32.6%). Voter turnout was 64.6% of 5.3 million registered voters. A few days before the second round, radical Islamists threatened terror attacks. But this could not be proven. Some observers questioned the origin of these threats, and suspected the involvement of the Ministry of the Interior in order to log roll the Nidaa Tounes candidate. Irrespective of this rumour, the presence of security forces was largely intensified during the election period all over the country. The second round took place on 21 December 2014. The duel between the two candidates left in the second round opposed Moncef Marzouki (CPR) and Beji Caid Essebsi (Nidaa Tounes). Finally, Beji Caid Essebsi was elected the first President of the 2nd Republic, with 55.68% of the votes, and officially took office on 31 December 2014. This victory of Beji Caid Essebsi, who presents himself as an inheritor of Bourguiba, can be understood as a sort of "soft restoration", as his party Nidaa Tounes includes former RCD members and

"Destourians" (supporters of Bourguiba's approach to state prestige and secular modernity).

The implementation of the first free and fair legislative and presidential elections, on the basis of the new constitution and the new electoral law, marked for the Tunisian political class the formal end of the transition phase and the beginning of the Second Republic of Tunisia. Now, the new institutions have to prove their effectiveness and the new constitution needs to be revitalised. On 5 January 2015 the new President Beji Caid Essebsi appointed Habib Essid as the new Prime Minister. The first proposal for the new government presented by Habib Essid was confronted with many critics from different political sides. Only the second proposal was accepted in February 2015, and the new government could start to work.

In addition to the democratic transition milestones described above, the role of civil society has been a very important factor for the successful implementation of these milestones.

The Role of Civil Society in the Transition Process

Throughout the whole transition phase, Tunisian civil society was and still is very active, and plays its role as a counter-power in the state. The room for action for civil society activists has widely increased since the revolution. In particular, Tunisian youths have been the "avant-garde of the revolution" (M'rad, 2014, p. 186). Civil society actors used the possibilities to make political pressure (e.g. Casbah1, Casbah2 in 2011) as well as concrete proposals within the political and constitutional process on different occasions (e.g. within the framework of the "National Dialogue"). Actually, the political crisis of 2013, after the assassination of the two opposition politicians Mohamed Brahmi and Chokri Belaid, has more or less been solved thanks to the commitment of civil society. Numerous human rights, women and youth activists, lawyers and trade unionists, organised peaceful demonstrations, created alternative platforms for political dialogue, and prevented a violent escalation of the political crisis.

The role of the trade union Union Générale des Travailleurs Tunisiens (UGTT) during the revolution was ambivalent: some trade unionists and local structures supported the revolution; however, the former UGTT leadership was partly rather close to the Ben Ali regime. After the revolution, the leadership team changed and the trade union played a constructive role in the transition process, especially within the framework of the National Dialogue. Conflicts with the Hamadi Jebali government had come up, when UGTT members had been attacked by Revolution Leagues in December 2012 (probably instigated by Ennahda). The UGTT asked for the dissolution of the Revolution Leagues and supported the idea of a technocrat government in early 2013. After the legislative and presidential elections of 2014, the UGTT called again for a participative economic dialogue and new salary negotiations for the public sector. Today, the UGTT represents a real opposition movement within the new political landscape, and has the capacity to mobilise many people.

The National Dialogue was mainly launched in spring 2013 in order to mediate between the Islamist faction and movement on the one hand, and the opposition faction and extra-parliamentarian opposition on the other. The so-called "Quartet" included the UGTT as principal mediator, as well as the employer's federation UTICA, the human rights organisation Ligue Tunisienne des Droits de l'Homme (LTDH), and the bar association (Ordre des avocats). In addition, representatives of the major political parties participated. A National Dialogue Roadmap (end of NCA, adoption of the constitution, elections) was established. After having played an important role in overcoming the political crisis of 2013, members of the national dialogue asked for an institutionalisation of this politico- societal platform.

Besides the UGTT, numerous human rights, lawyers, women and other civil society organisations were and still are very committed in pushing forward the transition process in their respective fields. Under the ancient regime, the possibilities for civil society activities were limited, and often restricted by censorship or repression. After the revolution, the room for manoeuvre for civil society organisations increased tremendously, and the number of civil society organisations exploded. The law for civil society organisations was facilitated and an unknown dynamic of civic commitment and new citizenship crossed the country. External actors and international donor institutions supported this dynamic and increased their financial support for civil society activities in Tunisia, also having an impact on the civil society landscape.

Tunisia has numerous factors that facilitate a democratic transition process, such as high education rates, liberal elites, a consensus-oriented tradition, an important broad and educated middle class, an active civil society and a moderate practice of Islam. The constellation of these factors renders the Tunisian democratic consolidation case specific and successfully contributed to achieving the constitution consensus. However, despite these favourable factors, the on-going transition process also has to face some challenges and difficulties.

Challenges and Difficulties

In terms of internal challenges, the Tunisian transition and democratic consolidation process has to cope with different problems such as the decomposition, fragmentation and tension between different political parties and camps, the phenomenon of political violence, the economic-financial and socioeconomic crisis, or the debate on a future societal consensus or inclusive society model allowing for the inclusion of all societal groups and factions.

Political and Institutional Transition, Good Governance, Transitional Justice

After the preparation and successful implementation of the legislative and presidential elections by the Instance supérieure indépendante pour les elections (ISIE), under the direction of Chafik Sarsar, effective political practice and good governance are the next challenges.

Different reforms in relation to the rule of law have already been tackled or implemented. This process continues and will include further constitutional amendments, legislation and decrees, in order to protect the constitutional state, especially the independence, professionalism and efficiency of the judiciary. In this domain, the rehabilitation of courts, fair access to justice and respect of fair trial standards or mechanisms in the transitional justice are on the agenda.In December 2014, the Association des Magistrats Tunisiens (AMT), organisation of the judges, asked the new government and new parliament to respect the new constitution and the constitutional organisations, to establish a republican, democratic-participatory system, securing the sovereignty of the law and the independence of jurisprudence. The AMT also asked for a fundamental revision of the Electoral Law and for more respect of deadlines by the parliament.

According to the Corruption Perceptions Index of Transparency International Tunisia has a score of 40/100, and lost 2 positions in 2014 in the ranking in comparison to 2013: Tunisia is now placed in position 79 of 175 countries.Transparency International calls upon the new government to take measures towards the further implementation of the United Nations Convention against Corruption, ratified by Tunisia in 2008. Amongst the obligations of this Convention are: the development of a national strategy to fight corruption in partnership with relevant parties, including civil society organisations, and enabling the National Anti-Corruption Commission to play its role effectively by providing financial support and qualified human resources.

A further challenge concerns the effective implementation of the guarantee of the respect for human rights as well as for freedom of press and expression. Therefore, Decree 115 on the media law, and Decree 116 on the Haute autorité indépendante de la communication audiovisuelle (HAICA) need to be effectively implemented, along with a reform of the penal code, constraining these freedoms. Many reforms and the creation of the aforementioned new control associations in terms of human rights, transparency and rule of law have been adopted. Now, these reforms and mechanisms will have to prove their effectiveness, such as the effective implementation of mechanisms of torture prevention. Actually, the situation of human rights has only partially improved since 2011. According to Amnesty International and other human rights organisations, human rights violations have continued since 2011. Torture has been used in prisons and in police stations, and security forces have continued to use excessive force against demonstrators.

In the field of women's rights, Tunisia was and is very advanced in terms of freedoms and gender equality compared to numerous European and MENA region countries. The Code du Statut personnel, guaranteeing important rights to women, has not been changed, although Ennahda tried to do so. The respect for women's rights has been reaffirmed by the lifting of key reservations on the UN Convention to Eliminate All Forms of Discrimination Against Women (CEDAW), ratified by Tunisia in 1985, and referred to as the international women's bill of rights. Tunisia officially notified the UN about lifting the reservations in April 2014, and is the first country in the region to remove all specific reservations to the treaty.However, women activists ask for further steps and for more systematic and efficient implementation of these principles and rights, for instance with regard to the inheritance law, which disadvantages women.

Other challenges consist of the local resilience to public policy reforms, pseudo-democratic acting by certain political representatives, sometimes an intentional delay of reforms, new corruption mechanisms and networks, a "revolution-exhausted" or reform-uninterested society, polarisation or fragmentation between different political poles. A climate of hate and threats emerged during the rule of Ennahda, especially in the social media, but also in public debates. However, this development has calmed down in the course of 2014.

Political Culture and Climate

While freedom of the press and freedom of expression have grown on the one hand, in the sense that less state censorship exists, and new media control associations and mechanisms have been developed, on the other, in daily life artists and intellectuals have increasingly become the target of physical attacks and/or psychological threats by Islamists. Different artists have been increasingly attacked, especially under the rule of Ennahda, but even afterwards. For instance, in June 2012, a contemporary art exhibition was attacked and destroyed by violent Salafists (Palais Adalliya, La Marsa). The different governments did not condemn these kinds of attacks, and did not push for criminal prosecution. In November 2014, a young rapper was kidnapped by radical Islamists, who forced him to cut his hair. Also in November 2014, UGTT leader Abassi was physically attacked by unknown persons, but not injured. At the same time, parts of the judiciary have not yet adapted to the new rights and freedoms, and sometimes react with disproportionate sentences, such as long-term imprisonments of bloggers for defamation of the army or state officials. But freedom of expression and press freedom might also be threatened anew because of the intensified "combat against terrorism", as the journalism union fears.

Although the disposition for political consensus is highly developed in Tunisia, in 2013, a rather strong polarisation emerged between an Islamist majority and a liberal opposition, in the NCA as in wider society. Two large factions continue to dominate the political debate: the defenders of a conservative "backlash" around Nida Tounes, and the Islamist faction around Ennahda. In between these two camps or around them, on their margins, the smaller leftist, liberal or progressive political groups or parties are more or less grounded or marginalised. But does it make sense to name these camps in terms of "Islamo-conservative" and "liberal-progressive", and to oppose a secular against a religious societal model? Do these notions really capture the social reality? In Tunisia, the Islam religion remains an important reference for the majority of the population. A certain social and religious conservatism is reality. But this majority believes in a moderate Islam. Political parties who use the religious reference can have major support from this large part of the society, as long as the political discourse remains moderate. At the same time, many mosques were and continue to be misused for political objectives, especially in times of electoral campaigns. According to the trade union of Imams, about 24 mosques are under the control of extremists and no longer under the control of the ministry. Another 85 mosques were privately built, are private property and are not under the control of the ministry.

Protests, strikes and physical attacks started in 2011 and actually continue since then, although on different scales. Strikes concern many different economic and professional sectors: e.g. workers in the textile industry and in the agricultural sector, employees of the transport society TRANSTU, or the personnel of hospitals. Even the employees of the Foreign Ministry once threatened a general strike. In Gafsa, a phosphate washing plant was closed for two years following protests. Many young people continue to protest because the new jobs and opportunities promised after 2011 were never created in these poorer regions in the centre of the country; but due to the continued protests the Tunisian phosphate production, once a market leader, decreased to a third of pre- revolution volumes, and business has shifted to regional competitors – a vicious circle.At different points of time during the last four years, the situation and climate within the society became very tense.

In terms of an open political debate, the two presidential candidates who were left for the second round, Beji Caid Essebsi ("the saviour") and Moncef Marzouki ("the victim") expressed a reciprocal hate tirade and controversial opinions just before the second round. The poising of the public debate went so far that the journalists' trade union even threatened to boycott the electoral campaign. On the other hand, civil society organisations such as the NGO Mourakiboun (Observateurs) intend to calm the spirits and help with electoral preparations and public debates. In 2014 and 2015, there have been several attacks of security forces against journalists. The journalist federation has criticised these attacks as a potential return to former repressive practices.

Facing increasing radical-Islamist terrorist threats (and some real attacks) in Tunisia, there is a great danger that the political class will fall back into the former security discourse and the security sector will re-intensify its observation and repression methods, practised by the Ben Ali regime and state security.

All these developments led to a political climate, where the majority of the population is tired of the revolution and protests. Daily life has become worse for many people, compared to their previous situation. Many people are somehow reluctant about reforms, disinterested or sobered. In reaction to the Bardo and Sousse terrorist attacks, large parts of the population are starting to support the new security discourse and security plans of the Nidaa Tounes government.

The Socioeconomic Challenge

Alongside the political, security and judicial reforms, the economic sector is in the middle of a fundamental transformation process. After decades of clientelism and kleptocracy under the Ben Ali regime, it is challenging to reinstall transparent conditions. Besides, a modernisation of the management of public funds is on the agenda. During the phase of the Troika government, critical voices against the Ennahda-led government became louder, questioning the economic and financial expertise of Ennahda policy makers in terms of re-establishing confidence of foreign investors and relaunching the Tunisian economy. Partially true, the argument was also used to weaken the Ennahda party, and to put in place a technocrat-led government afterwards.

After the first shock of the revolution in 2011, the economy broke down (-2%), then, economic growth recovered again with 3% in 2012, but went down again afterwards. Despite the political turbulences in the aftermath of the Tunisian revolution, the majority of international and European enterprises present in Tunisia remained. Out of 1,200 French enterprises only about 30 left the country (Bauchard, 2013, p. 5). Important economic and social reforms are on the agenda, some of them meeting resistance amongst the concerned professional sectors or the broader consumer society. In particular, the labour market is concerned, especially in terms of youth unemployment. Since 2011 unemployment rates have remained very high: the official unemployment rate is 15.2% (2014); youth unemployment is between 30% and 40% depending on the region; and graduate unemployment is 31.4% (2014).After a phase of relative calm, protests in the public sector and other economic sectors returned in 2014.

Tunisia is an upper middle income country, and has a population of about 10.89 million inhabitants (2013), a GDP of 46.99 billion USD (2013). Infant mortality is decreasing: 13 (per 1000 live births, 2013), life expectancy of 74 years (2013), and adult literacy rates of 89% (male) and 74 % (female) (2015), and the GNI per capita is 4200 USD (2013).

According to recent IMF and World Bank Reports Tunisia is developing despite a difficult regional context. However, 2015 will be a difficult year and expectations should not be too high; the economic situation remains difficult. Growth rates remain fragile (2.3% in 2015, 2.4% in 2014, 2.3% in 2013)added to high unemployment and a highly informal economy, which has grown since 2011 (estimated at 50% of GDP); but the predictions for growth were 3% for 2015 and 4.1% for 2016.Public debt is estimated at 51.7% of GDP in 2014, and 53% of GDP in 2015. Foreign investments are decreasing (2014: 12.5% less than in 2013; 22.3% less than in 2010); the household deficit will increase (+1%). Foreign investors hesitate to invest in Tunisia because of the unstable regional and political context. The recent terrorist attacks of March and June 2015 will negatively impact on the tourism sector and foreign investment. In the Doing Business 2015 Ranking of the World Bank, Tunisia came 60th (2015) against 56th (2014).

The negative score of the commercial balance has increased (2013: - 12.8%; 2014: - 13.3% of GDP). In 2014, exports increased by only 2.5%, while imports increased by 6.4%. The public budget deficit decreased (6.8% in 2013) to 5% of the GDP in 2014.Salaries do not increase in the same manner as the price levels. Since 2010, the average salary increased by 17%; but the price index for households by 21.5%. Food and beverages increased by 27.2%. The health care system remains in difficulties. The trade unions threaten with strikes in hospitals against the decisions of the health ministry to cut the budget for primary healthcare by 17%. Regional imbalances persist between the rich capital and its surroundings and the coastal regions on the one hand, and the poorer regions in the centre and in the south on the other. The poor and needy population is estimated at 3 million. The social security system is in deficit (-345 million TND).While the general school enrolment rate is high (99% of children aged 6-11), poverty remains at about 15% on average, and 32% in certain regions (Centre-West, South-West).

The tourism sector, vital for the Tunisian economy and representing 7.3% of Tunisian GDP, collapsed in 2011, and it took a while to recover. But the sector never reached pre 2011 levels again. The two terrorist attacks of 18 March 2015 (22 deaths) and 26 June 2015 (38 deaths) harmed the sector even more. 470,000 direct and indirect jobs (14% of the active population) depend on tourism.In reaction to the Bardo Museum attack, the number of tourists decreased by 25.7% in April 2015 and the foreign currency revenues decreased by 26.3%, according to the Central Bank.A broad tourism campaign made hotel reservations climb slightly again, from 39.4% to 44.9% in Mai 2015.But the number of French tourists decreased so much (-37.7% compared to May 2014) that for the first time the number of British tourists was higher in 2015 than the number of French tourists, traditionally number one.After the brutal attack in Sousse on 26 June 2015, the summer vacation season 2015 was heavily affected, and different tour operators cancelled their trips. The attack in Sousse has not only harmed the tourism image and sector of Tunisia, but also foreign investments in general. Tunisia has desperately tried to attract new foreign investments since 2011. All are aware that a re-launch of the economy is a pre-condition for the success of the political democratic transition process. That was exactly the target of the Islamic State – to destabilise the transition process.

The Financial Law for 2015 allocates 15% of the budget alone for the ministries of the Interior (2.6 billion TND, for 3,000 new security officers, among others) and of Defence (1.8 billion TND, for 8000 new soldiers, among others), as well as an increase of the budget for the Presidency, the Parliament and less for the Prime Minister. Both ministries (Interior and Defence) intend to buy expensive anti-terrorism equipment. For 2015, another increase in electricity and gas prices (7%) is planned.

Further points on the economic and financial agenda are the reform of the fiscal system, a better distribution of wealth in society, an increase of the minimum wage, and an improvement in labour rights according to international standards (ILO). Last but not least, Tunisia remains committed to further regional integration of the Maghreb region.

Next to the named challenges to the Tunisian transition, different additional factors render the situation more difficult, such as the negative impacts of the Libyan civil war on Tunisia, and the negative impact of transnational radical Islamism (international and domestic terrorism) on Tunisia.

The Security Challenge

With regard to the security situation, different threats can be identified: the impact of the Libyan conflict, activities of radical extremists at the border with Algeria and Libya, activities of radicalised Syrian return fighters,and radical Salafists on a domestic level (home-grown terrorism). The general security situation in the country is calm, but in some parts of the country, radical individuals and groups succeeded in spreading violence and insecurity, especially in the border zones with Libya and Algeria, where armed Jihadist groups are active, or in the mountains of Jbel Chambi. Several soldiers and police officers have been killed since 2013 in fights with these groups. After a phase of institutional silence, the Tunisian government installed special military zones at the borders. The number of these fighters remains unclear.

Major shocks in terms of new security threats and deliberate provocation were the attacks against European tourists in the Bardo Museum of Tunis on 18 March 2015 (22 death) and in El Kantaoui – Sousse on 26 June 2015 (38 deaths), claimed by the Islamic State. But the attack of the United States Embassy and the American School of Tunis (ACST) in September 2012 by radical Salafists (Ansar Al-Sharia), announced an increasing impact of international and home-grown violent Jihadism in Tunisia. At the time, the Ennahda-led government did not react instantly, and the police came very late, accused of being indulgent with the radical Islamists. Ansar Al-Sharia is the armed branch of the Salafist movement; it is a radical Jihadist movement, originally created as a charity association, and founded by Abou Ayad. Today, it has about 10,000 estimated followers, and its radicalised Jihadist fighters are active in Syria, Algeria, and the Sahel region. Most of their arms come from Libya. The radical Salafist movement is also held responsible for numerous attacks against artists, intellectuals, students and professors (e.g. in Manouba University). They are also accused of the murder of Chokri Belaid and Mohamed Brahmi, and were formally labelled a "terrorist organisation" in 2013 by the Ministry of the Interior.

Since 2014, physical attacks, arrests or armed conflicts between the Tunisian police, military, security forces and radical fighters have taken place almost every day. For instance, in 2014, smaller terrorist cells were arrested in Sousse/Kalaat Al-Koubra (Al Nousra group), accused of being involved in the planned attacks prior to the recent elections. In December 2014, a policeman of the Garde nationale was killed (and beheaded) in Le Kef, by about 15 terrorists. He was not armed, as he was not in service at the time. Also in December 2014, a trial took place against a group of presumed terrorists of Ansar Al-Sharia, accused of having killed a state trooper during an armed attack against the border guard in Jbel Bouchebka in January 2014. The families of the accused Jihadists seem to receive money from Abou Ayadh, who is planning to establish a Tunisian branch of IS. Journalists were not allowed to follow this process. In Kasserine, five people were arrested as presumed terrorists who had helped the groups hiding in Jbel Chaambi. A further eight soldiers were killed in Jbel Chaambi in summer 2013, by a group called Okba Ibn Nafaa.

The external influence of radical Salafism is increasing. In 2011, the number of radical Salafists was estimated at only 200. This number rapidly increased in the aftermath of the revolution and the general complexity of the upheaval. The open border situation with Libya facilitated the entry for radical Jihadists into

Tunisia, and all Islamist political prisoners who had been in prison under the Ben Ali regime were released. It is estimated that about 2,000 Tunisian Jihadists are currently fighting for the IS in Syria, among them a Tunisian terrorist, Kamel Zarrouk (Ansar Al-Sharia). These fighters represent an additional risk when they return to Tunisia.

A reform of the security sector, especially with regard to the police and border controls, has been on the agenda since 2011, but has not really been tackled so far.

Negative Impact of the Libyan Crisis

An increasing export of terror from Libya toward the whole Maghreb region is taking place. IS plans to establish a structure for the African continent in the Maghreb, in Libya. The plan is to train fighters in Libya and to distribute instructions and commands from Libya to the other Maghreb countries. It is presumed that the Tunisian Ansar Al-Sharia works together with IS. The Tunisian government is explicitly against a military intervention

in Libya. It does not want to cooperate with the terrorist militias, but recognises the two currently existing rival governments in Libya: an Islamist government in Tripoli, and a government of Abdallah Al-Thani in Tobruk, recognised by the international community, and under the protection of General Khalifa Haftar, controlling the eastern part of the country), and proposes new methods for the anti-terrorism combat. Many Tunisian citizens still live and work in Libya, and an evacuation of these citizens is under discussion. Two Tunisian journalists have been kidnapped in Libya.

In 2014, many Libyans continue to live in Tunisia, having fled the civil war in their country. This presence also implies additional socioeconomic problems for Tunisia. Housing rents went up due to increased demands. Additional food, logistical, health and other services become necessary. Libyan children need to be integrated into the Tunisian school system, and workers integrated into the labour market. Many injured people from Libya come to hospitals in Tunisia. Armed fights between the Libyan army and militias at the Libyan- Tunisian border take place more often, and paralyse the border region around the border crossing of Ras Jedir.

Conclusion and Perspectives

In sum, the challenges for consolidating a democratic system in Tunisia are still numerous and multifaceted. The future developments will largely depend on the interplay and cooperation between the new political majorities and the opposition, on the implementation of the new constitution, but also on the development of the regional environment, the support by the international community, and last but not least on the resilience to financial and economic pressures and security threats.

In terms of political freedoms, there has been an important liberalisation after the fall of the Ben Ali regime. In particular, the media is less controlled, and the freedom of opinion and freedom of expression have increased. The political climate has changed and developed. The results of the legislative and presidential elections in 2014 showed that the newly emerging Tunisian political system has succeeded in practising a peaceful political alternance, in a pluralistic political party system. New alliances between political parties came up after the electoral success of Nidaa Tounes in October 2014. It remains to be seen if the influence of former regime representatives and followers in this party hinder further reforms and political liberalisation, or whether there might be a step backwards in terms of political transition and transformation. Tunisia is far away from an Egyptian scenario, including a military and authoritarian backlash, but the danger of a (neo)conservative roll-back exists. The accentuation of a transnational, regional and domestic Islamist-terrorist threat, in order to push forward security measures, sometimes recalls the discourses of the Ben Ali regime. The new democratic institutions are challenged to provide respect for human rights and fundamental freedoms, and to be able to guarantee the independence of justice.

Irrespective of these politically contentious issues, there are further steps ahead, especially in terms of economic governance, such as the step-by-step introduction of a social market economy, the development of a just and committed social policy addressing all social categories and regions, a modernisation of the economic structures (innovation and reorientation towards future-oriented economic sectors), an increase of the level of economic competition, the development of the private sector and its good governance, improvement of the general business climate and the fostering of public-private partnerships.

According to different international indices, the democratic consolidation process in Tunisia is advanced in terms of democracy, good governance and human rights, and especially in terms of ratification and signatures of international conventions. Tunisia has many trump cards for a consolidated democratisation process: committed elites, an important middle class, committed civil society, a social acquis, a viable education

system and important human capital, and last but not least an important disposition for political compromise and consensus finding. Tunisia is in the middle of reinventing its political system and society project. Inclusion of the different political factions and societal groups will be one of the keys, alongside a fair and transparent distribution of prosperity, social cohesion, employment, transitional justice, security, development of the poorer regions and professional future perspectives for the young generation.

Lightning Source UK Ltd.
Milton Keynes UK
UKHW020643291221
396330UK00011B/671